The A to Z of Restoration London

(The City of London, 1676)

Introductory Notes by
Ralph Hyde

Index Compiled by
John Fisher and Roger Cline

LONDON TOPOGRAPHICAL SOCIETY
Publication No. 145
1992

ISBN 0 902087 32 0

Printed in Great Britain by Headley Brothers Ltd The Invicta Press Ashford Kent and London

CONTENTS

To His most Sacred Matie CHARLES II.
To His Royal Confort our moft gracious Queen CATHERINE
And to the moft Illuftrious Prince and Princefs
JAMES and MARY Duke and Duchefs of YORK etc.^{a}

Whofe bounty encouraged Mr OGILBY to begin the Actual Survey of
ENGLAND whereof this being part is moft rightfully and humbly
dedicated By their Majefties and Royal Highneffes moft dutiful
and obedient Servant

WILLIAM MORGAN His Majefties COSMOGRAPHER

To His Royal Highnefs
James D. of York etc.^{a}

To Her Royal Highnefs
Mary Duchefs of York etc.^{a}

To His Highnefs
The Prince of Orange

To the Lady Anne
2.^{d} Dau.^{r} to his Royall Highnefs

To Her Highnefs
The Princefs of Orange etc.^{a}

To His Highnefs
Prince Rupert etc.^{a}

To His Highnefs
The Prince Palatine etc.^{a}

John Ogilby hands to Charles II the subscription book for *Britannia*, the projected multi-volumed atlas which would include the survey of the City of London. Detail from William Morgan's 'London Actually Survey'd', 1682. (Reproduced by Courtesy of the Museum of London).

OGILBY AND MORGAN'S CITY OF LONDON MAP, 1676[†]

The need

The Great Fire of London began in Pudding Lane close to the north end of London Bridge on 2 September 1666. By the time the fire was brought under control four days later, 13,000 houses, the Royal Exchange, the Custom House, 44 Livery Company halls, the Guildhall, St Paul's Cathedral, 87 parish churches, and furniture and commodities valued at over £3,500,000 in the currency of the time, had been destroyed. Two thirds of the City of London lay in smouldering ruins.

Ogilby and Morgan's large-scale map of the City was completed and published ten years later. It shows the new City as built – not an ideal City with straight streets and noble vistas such as Christopher Wren had initially envisaged, but a fairly practical, improved City, the best that could be sensibly hoped for, with wider streets, buildings of brick or stone, markets removed from main thoroughfares, the Fleet River dredged, and hints of an intended Thames embankment.

Maps after the Great Fire were going to be vital, and the monarch was a man who understood their utility. Four days after the Great Fire Charles II informed the Lord Mayor and aldermen that he had appointed Wenceslaus Hollar and Francis Sandford to make an exact plan and survey of the City 'as it now stands.' The City Fathers were commanded to give the mapmakers every assistance. The King also encouraged Hollar to complete his 'Great Map of London', a multi-sheet map-view, begun in 1658 and eventually abandoned. And when on 6 March 1667 the City Corporation submitted its proposals for rebuilding the City, the King returned them with the instruction that the information should be plotted onto a map.

The map that Charles needed on 6 March 1667 was supplied six days later. In all probability it was the six-sheet manuscript skeleton survey that the City had commissioned almost immediately after the Great Fire, and which had been undertaken in December 1666 by a team of able surveyors – John Leake, John Jennings, William Marr, William Leybourn, Thomas Streete, and Richard Shortgrave. (A single-sheet manuscript reduction of the Leake's map is preserved in the British Library). On this were shown the sites of the public buildings, the outline of the streets with widths at various important places, and one or two projected improvements. Such maps would be needed at Guildhall, and at Whitehall too, by departments, committees, and individuals involved in planning

and rebuilding the City. The cumbersomely-named Committee of the Common Council Touching the Affair of Rebuilding the City directed a stationer, Major Nathaniel Brooke, to engrave and publish a two-sheet reduction from the six-sheet draft. Hollar was engaged to engrave it. For the districts lying beyond the burnt area of the City he seems to have made full use of his never-to-be-completed 'Great Map.' Other mapmakers – John Overton and William Dunster, for instance – were keen to publish plans showing the extent of the Fire. On 7 May the Court of Aldermen prohibited 'them and all others to make and publish such maps ...' The prohibition was ignored: Overton and Robert Pricke published Fire maps regardless. Nathaniel Brooke brought a petition against a certain Thomas Rookes 'concerning making and publishing a map, and also for abetting and encouraging Robert Horne, bookseller, using the same sign as Brooke', successfully it would seem, for no trace of a London map by Rookes has been located.

As reconstruction got under way, the map that was really needed by the City administrators was one drawn carefully to scale that showed every individual building within the City as well as those immediately bordering it. The mapmaker who set himself to provide the City with what it needed was John Ogilby.

John Ogilby and the 'Britannia' project

At the time of the Great Fire John Ogilby was a successful translator and publisher working in Whitefriars, south of Fleet Street. He was born in 1600 in Kirriemuir, about fifteen miles north of Dundee. By 1606 the Ogilby family had moved to London where the father had run up heavy debts. Young Ogilby was apprenticed to a dancer. In 1621, whilst performing in a masque before James I he broke a leg. This brought his dancing career to an abrupt end, and caused him to limp thereafter. On 6 July 1629 he was made free of the Worshipful Company of Merchant Taylors. Three years later he opened his own dancing school opposite Gray's Inn. For several years he served as Viscount Wentworth's dancing master in Dublin. He established a theatre in St Werburgh Street, and in 1638 was appointed Master of the King's Revels in Ireland. In 1641 his fortunes declined: Wentworth was executed, and Ogilby's theatre closed. In about 1647 he returned to England

almost penniless. In 1651 he married, and shortly afterwards moved to a house in King's Head Court, Shoe Lane. He acquired a knowledge of Latin, and soon put this accomplishment to use by translating Virgil and Aesop's *Fables*. He also received lessons in Greek, and having mastered that language published in 1660 a verse translation of Homer's *Iliad*, adorned with engravings by Wenceslaus Hollar 'and other eminent engravers.' On the accession of Charles II Ogilby was instantly in royal favour. He was ordered to compose the poetical parts for the procession that took place on the day before the Coronation, and record the occasion in a lavish volume, which he published, *The Relation of the Entertainment of His Majesty Charles II, in his Passage through the City of London to his Coronation*. He was reappointed in 1661 Master of the King's Revels in Ireland; and was granted in 1665 a privilege which protected his books against piracy for fifteen years. During the Great Fire he suffered a new catastrophe. His house in Whitefriars was destroyed, and his entire stock of books too. He was left with only £5.0s.0d. Despite this daunting setback he was soon re-established, rebuilding his house and once more engaging assistants. It was at this point that he turned his attention to the production and publication of elaborate geographical volumes.

On 10 May 1669 Ogilby issued proposals for a five-volumed *English Atlas*, covering Africa, America, Asia, Europe, and Great Britain. Over the next few years Ogilby was constantly fine-tuning the project. Priority, he announced in June 1670, would be given to Great Britain. In November 1671 he promised that Great Britain – 'Britannia' was the name he gave to this section – would contain road maps and a map of each county. In about February 1672 he issued a new prospectus, 'Mr. Ogilby's Design for Carrying on his Britannia.' 'Britannia' would now consist of six volumes. Four of them would be devoted to geographical and historical description of England and Wales and be illustrated with county maps. Volume five would be an ichnographical and historical description of all the principal roadways of England and Wales. Ichnographical was the term then used for plans, distinguishing them from map-views. The *grand finale* would be 'A New and Accurate Description of the famous City of London, with the perfect Ichnography thereof, according to its Six and Twenty Wards, in a fair large Volume illustrated with the Scenography of all Eminent Buildings and Places belonging thereunto.' This would be accompanied by four large maps of England, a plan of the City of London, and another of the City of Westminster, 'curiously and accurately performed beyond whatever has yet been attempted for any city of the Universe.' The description of London would cost subscribers £5.0s.0d, the surveys of London and Westminster an extra £4.0s.0d.

Portrait of John Ogilby (1600–1676), by P. Lombart after Sir Peter Lely. (Reproduced by courtesy of Guildhall Library.)

The City of London survey

In Ogilby's 'Design for Carrying on His Britannia' we learn that Charles II had granted Ogilby the authority to carry out the survey of England and Wales, that he had referred the 'design' to certain lords of the Privy Council for their inspection, and that he had taken out a subscription for £500.0s.0d for himself, and a further £500.0s.0d for his consort, Queen Katherine of Braganza. Useful support came from the Royal Exchange's governing body, the Gresham Committee, which in March 1670 allotted him a vacant shop in the Exchange at ground floor level in which to show off his various volumes, particularly Africa of the *English Atlas*, which had just been (or was just about to be) published. Regular support for the *English Atlas* came from the Court of Aldermen of the City of London. On 28 July 1670, for example, they instructed the Chamberlain of London to pay Ogilby £20.0s.0d as a gratuity for Africa. On 18 October 1670, having received the volume for the Empire of Japan from him, 'for the encouragement of his studies' they presented him with a further £20.0s.0d. On 2 May 1671 they gave him £20.0s.0d for his 'Atlas Chinensis'. And on 12 December 1671 they gave him yet another £20.0s.0d for America. Ogilby responded to the City's support by embarking on his survey of the

City, and giving the City map – a relatively small part of the overall design – special priority.

By early 1672 he had told the Corporation what he was up to. His was going to be 'the most accurate Survey of the City of London and Libertyes thereof than hitherto hath been done.' It would be accompanied by a description. No systematic description of London, it should be noted, had been attempted since John Stow's in Tudor times.

Ogilby had no difficulty in persuading the City Fathers that they needed a dependable large-scale survey. The reconstruction of the City was now well under way. It was no longer a desolate territory of rubble and staked-out foundations. Large numbers of new houses had been erected, Edward Jarman's new Royal Exchange had been completed, and the building of new churches had been authorised by the second Rebuilding Act of 1670. A new civic pride was abroad. The map would be an invaluable tool for the administrators at Guildhall. But it would have a second function. As a large spectacular wall map it would broadcast to the world that the City was back in business. Ogilby asked the aldermen for the City's co-operation and he got it. 'John Ogilby', they instructed, 'shall proceed in the said Worke without interrupcioun or molestacioun of any other person or persons that shall or may attempt the same design.'

The surveyor Ogilby appointed to take charge of the City of London map was William Leybourn (1626-1716). Leybourn at 46 was renowned as a writer on mathematics and on the theory and practice of surveying. His first book, a joint work with a fellow surveyor, Vincent Wing, was *Urania Practica, or, Practical Astonomie*. His next work, *Planometrica: or, the Whole Art of Surveying of Land*, was published under the anagramatic pseudonym of Oliver Wallinby in 1650. In 1653, at the age of 27, he improved on this small work by publishing *The Compleat Surveyor*, a book so successful that it passed through four editions in his life and one after. In 1666 he proved his practical capabilities when, with five other surveyors, he carried out the post-Fire survey of the City. The vast survey of the City which he carried out for Ogilby, however, was without any doubt, his greatest practical achievement. He did not do it single-handed. He was assisted, we know, by John Holwell, who measured and plotted over 200 acres (81 hectares) of the area covered by the map, by Gregory King, and no doubt by others. When King joined the team he was not especially impressed by what was going on. In his autobiographical notes he wrote:

> At Mr. King's coming to Mr. Ogilby, he found Mr Leyburn just newly Engaged in making a Map of London, and viewing the first Essay of that Survey, he found it was projected at a Scale of 50 feet to an Inch and yet particularized nothing but only yᵉ Streets Lanes etc. Whereupon Mr. King formed a New Project of that Survey at 100 feet per Inch, and expressed the groundplots of every individual house and Garden, finisht 2 plates of 20 himself, and Ordered the carrying on of the rest of the work ...

The Description was also progressing. On 3 June 1673 the Court of Aldermen declared itself well satisfied with it. Ogilby asked the Court for a subscription 'for his better enablement to proceed in the said work.' The Court ordered the Chamberlain to pay him the sum of £100 more when the work was completed to their satisfaction. In return for this promise of financial assistance, though, the aldermen insisted in having all drafts vetted by a committee appointed by themselves. The members of this committee were named in an order issued by William Wagstaffe, the Town Clerk, a few days later. They were: Alderman Sir William Turner, Lord Mayor in 1668-1669 and a Past Master of Ogilby's own Livery Company, the Merchant Taylors; Alderman Sir Richard Ford, Lord Mayor in 1670-1671; Alderman Sir Robert Vyner, a man of legendary wealth who would serve as Lord Mayor in 1674-1675; Alderman Sir Thomas Davies, to whom the index to the survey would be dedicated; John Dryden's 'railing Rabshekah', Sir Thomas Player, Chamberlain of London; and

Portrait of William Leybourn (1626–1716), by R. White. (Reproduced by courtesy of Guildhall Library.)

the City Surveyor, Robert Hooke. The order urged the Companies and corporations of the City, and all worthy citizens, to support 'a Work so generally Useful and Necessary' by taking out liberal subscriptions and making contributions. For its part, the Corporation would lead the way with a subscription of £200.0s.0d.

By the end of the year the first of the draft sheets for the plan had been drawn. On 8 December Ogilby showed it to Robert Hooke. The occasion is recorded in Hooke's diary. A second sheet was drawn in January 1674. Hooke inspected it at Garraway's Coffee House, and wrote a report for Ogilby to the Court of Aldermen. On 29th the two men met at Guildhall to discuss the map, and on 13 March Hooke wrote an address for him to the Justices at Hicks Hall, the session house at Clerkenwell. On 4 March they met at the Spanish Coffee House, Hooke giving Ogilby a hand to draft an address to the Merchant Taylors.

It is clear from these entries in Hooke's diary that although progress was being made on the City survey, Ogilby was not receiving the amount of financial support he needed to complete the map quickly. The vetting committee inspected specimens for the Description and the map and were impressed. Ogilby must have stressed his urgent need for support. In their report to the Court the committee members recommended a new appeal to the 'Companies and Fraternities of the City, and all other persons of Quality and Merchants, Inhabitants thereof ...' Their recommendation was accepted. On 10 February 1674 the Court of Aldermen issued another appeal on the lines suggested.

The map is completed

In the 1674 edition of Leybourn's *Compleat Surveyor*, the author describes his survey of the City then in progress. 'This Last is now under my hands', he writes, 'and I hope with God's assistance in a few months time to compleat it.' The survey, in actual fact, did not appear on the market until January 1677, three years later. The reason for this was not simply lack of support for this particular venture. The whole of the 'Britannia' project was suffering from lack of financial encouragement. Ogilby was obliged to tailor it. He announced in 1675 a new and smaller project. This, in some respects, was a more manageable and better balanced scheme than its predecessors, for it now included a series of town plans. In the preface to the volume of road maps, which appeared in 1675, Ogilby announced that 'Britannia' would consist of only three volumes – the road book itself; a 'Description of the 25 Cities with Peculiar Charts of each of them, but more particularly those of London and Westminster'; and a volume containing 'A Topographical

Description of the Whole Kingdom.' This Triple Illustration of the Kingdom', as he termed it, is represented by Hollar on the engraved title-page of the road book by three lively putti bearing scrolls: on the first scroll is a strip road map, on the second a minute plan of London, and on the third a county map of Yorkshire. The cruel fact was that the massive financial support so crucial for the 'Britannia's' progress was not materialising. Good will was also in decline. And yet despite the shortage of capital, and the ignorance and malice of his detractors alluded to in the road book's preface, Ogilby was still optimistic. For a work of such manifest utility, universal acceptance was inevitable.

A variety of maps, plans, and descriptions – all fragments of the great 'Britannia' project (in turn only part of the very much greater *English Atlas* project) – were now planned, in hand, or actually materialising. County maps of Kent and Middlesex were being engraved when Gregory King joined Ogilby's staff, and Robert Felgate was about to survey Essex. King joined him, helping him with the surveying and compiling notes for the written description in which the map was intended to appear. In the middle of the year, in

Engraved title-page to Volume 1 of *Britannia.* (Reproduced by courtesy of *The Map Collector.*)

'very severe cold weather', they carried out large-scale surveys of Ipswich and Maldon, which afterwards were 'very curiously finished and sent to those two places.' Surveys of Carlisle, Newcastle, Berwick, and possibly King's Lynn were planned, and intending donors of plates promised dedications and inscriptions. After working for a while with Leybourn on the City of London survey, and assisting with the 'Britannia' road book, King, with Felgate, embarked in the spring of 1674 on a survey of Westminster on the same scale as the survey of the City – 100 feet to an inch. Whilst it was in progress he lodged with a Mrs Anne Powell in St James's Street, Covent Garden, whom he subsequently married. The 'Britannia' road book, as we have seen, was published in 1675, the Description of London was progressing to the satisfaction of the aldermen, and the twenty plates for the City of London survey were being engraved by Wenceslaus Hollar and other engravers. In an advertisement in the *London Gazette* on 20-24 April 1676, Ogilby announced that the map of London would be 'suddenly finished', and warned subscribers that counterfeits were in preparation. No map should be received that did not have Ogilby's name on it, and the title of 'His Majesties Cosmographer.'

But on 4 September he died. Ogilby's widow, Christian, inherited his estate; William Morgan, his step-grandson, inherited the unenviable task of completing 'Britannia' which he hoped (in his will) would be to Morgan's 'great advantage.' Nervous subscribers, conscious perhaps of the shaky state of the over-stretched Ogilby enterprise, needed reassurance. On 12-16 October Morgan placed an advertisement in the *London Gazette* confidently stating that the *English Atlas* would be continued and finished. The large map of the City of London had been completed, he told them, and would be exposed for sale next term (i.e. Hilary Term, beginning 11 January).

The City of London survey, its twenty sheets in all probability joined together, backed with linen, mounted on rollers, and hung as a wall map, was exposed before the Court of Aldermen on 26 October. The Court seems to have been impressed. It awarded Morgan £100.0.s.0d. The aldermen expected, nevertheless – and this expectation was actually minuted – that each of them would get a free copy.

Publication of the map was announced in the *London Gazette* on 25-29 January 1677:

> Mr. Ogilby's Large Map of London accurately Survey'd at 100 Foot to an Inch, being finish'd by his Kinsman William Morgan, His Majesty's Cosmographer, is Sold at his House at White-Friars, Mr. Isted in Fleetstreet, Mr. Pask under the North-side of the Royal Exchange, Mr. Richards at the Golden Ball in Cornhil, Mr. Green at the Rose and Crown in Budge-row, and Mr. Berry at the Globe in Charing-cross.

A rather slovenly-compiled index to the plan was published in the form of a small volume with the title, *London Survey'd:, or, an Explanation of the Large Map of London.*

Reliability of the City of London survey

Ogilby's City of London map represents very nearly the first linear ground plan (or 'plot' to use the contemporary term) of a British town. It was certainly the first large, multi-sheet plan of a British town to be drawn in this manner. The early London maps – the 'copper plate map' of *c.*1553 and its derivatives, Faithorne and Newcourt's map of 1658, and even the far more sophisticated 'Great Map' of Wenceslaus Hollar – were all in reality map-views, depicting each building in bird's-eye fashion whilst maintaining, as far as was practicable, a constant scale throughout. The earlier method of map delineation had certain merits. It allowed the mapmaker to exhibit a wealth of topographical detail which his successors were obliged to ignore. The maker had to be artist; the products of his labours were documents of considerable charm. On the other hand the method allowed him to disguise his ignorance of topographical detail as well as his knowledge of it. As John Holwell observed in his *Sure Guide* ..., 'Those that are minded to draw the Map of any Town, City, or Corporation, only with the Uprights of the Houses, will have no need to measure either the House, Courts, or Allies thereof.' It was inevitable that Ogilby, moving in the same circle as Hooke, Wren, and Flamsteed, daily coming into contact with Fellows of the Royal Society, should have adopted the most mathematically precise and scientific surveying methods.

The surveying methods used by Ogilby's surveyors are fairly well documented. Leybourn, in the second edition of his *Compleat Surveyor*, published in 1674 when the City survey was in progress, inserted a second part to the fourth book in order to describe for the first time 'the manner of measuring and Plotting of Roads, Highways, Streets, Lanes, &c. and to take the Ichnography or Ground-plot of Cities, Towns, Hamlets, &c.' The plotting of streets in towns, he tells us, calls for far more exactness than is necessary for strip road maps, for example, for being on a larger scale, every small bowing, though it make not an angle of above 3 or 4 degrees, must be taken notice of.' The theodolite or semi-circle was more apt for this than the circumferentor, 'yet in this you need not with your instrument make observation of these small Angles, but having made observation of 4 eminent angles and the principal intermedial ones, you may by the help of Rods or Bevels for that purpose more accurately find the quantity of those breaks and angles.' Leybourn explains the

way in which principal streets are to be surveyed, then bye-lanes, and finally courts, alleys, and eminent houses. The information must be recorded, he says, in a book, and when complete transferred into the map. 'And thus having taken one part or quarter of a Town or City, you may proceed to another, and so on after another till you finish what you intended to have a plot of. This is the best and most accurate way that I can prescribe for the Plotting of Cities or Towns', Leybourn concludes, 'and it is the way that I my self use in my survey of the City of London which in now Reedified, wherein I take notice of all remarkable things therein; For besides the High streets and streets of note, I take notice of, and Plot, all Bye-streets and Lanes, all Courts and Allies, all Churches and Church-yards, and the 2 Temples, and all Inns of Court, all Colledges, the Guild-hall, and all eminent Halls of Corporations, all Market houses, &c.'

John Holwell, in his *Sure Guide to the Practical Surveyor* published in 1678, devotes the second part of his textbook to 'The Mesuration and Plotting of Streets, Lanes, Courts, and Allies, with the drawing of a Ground-Plott of all Houses, Churches, and Eminent Places of any City or Corporation.' His account is long, involved, and, though intended for the beginner, not easy to follow. 'In this manner', he concludes, 'is the City of London surveyed by John Ogilby Esquire, I myself being concerned in Measuring and Plotting above 200 acres thereof. This is the best and most accurate way that I can find out in all my Practice; one day's experience will confirm any one in my Opinion.'

The City of Ogilby and Morgan

By the time Leybourn and his assistants had completed the survey, the City was almost entirely rebuilt. In place of rickety half-timbered houses of pre-Fire days, the streets were lined with rows of regulation houses. The streets themselves were straighter and wider. Such thoroughfares as Thames Street and Threadneedle Street no longer dwindled to a bare eleven feet from house front to house front. The approach to London Bridge down Gracechurch Street and Fish Street Hill was opened up to thirty-five feet. The west entry through Ludgate from St Bride's to St Paul's was widened to forty feet. A minimum of fourteen feet was allotted to lanes and side streets – sufficient to allow two drays to pass; Ironmongers Lane has maintained the post-Fire regulation widths to the present day. Leading up to Guildhall a new street was created – Queen Street and King Street. Besides providing a useful approach this street relieved pressure on Dowgate and Queenhithe, and its popularity is demonstrated on the map by the number of boats clustered around the

stairs. Traffic flow was also helped by shifting the markets from the main streets. Cheapside Market was moved to Honey Lane, a new square was created for Newgate Market, the Stocks Market was erected on the site of St Mary Woolchurch, and more ground acquired for Leadenhall.

The general rebuilding of the burnt churches was begun in 1670 when the second Rebuilding Act was passed, removing the uncertainty as to which would be suppressed. Thirty temporary buildings ('tabernacles') were provided for worship for the returning population; these were usually put up in churchyards, but some were the old churches with temporary roofs. Only half of the new Wren churches had been, or were being, constructed when Ogilby and Morgan finished off their map in 1676: several were not constructed till the 1690s. The churches that are shown on the map in many cases were still waiting for their towers and spires, these being added, once the parishes could afford them, some of them in the early 18th century. St Paul's Cathedral, begun in June 1675, was not completed till 1710. Its ground plan is shown on the map drawn to scale and in some detail. Ogilby, we may suspect, conferred with Wren. Nevertheless the cathedral's plan does not conform with that adopted; in fact the west end of it corresponds with Wren's discarded Warrant Design.

Of the forty-four Livery Company halls destroyed in the Fire, forty-one were rebuilt, some being new halls, others old halls patched up. By 1676 most of them were in use again, but it was not until 1685 that the buildings were completed and the Companies housed in their old state. Of the City institutions, Sion College and Library were rebuilt by 1670, Blackwell Hall and the Custom House by 1671, the north block of the College of Arms by 1673, and enough of Christ's Hospital to accommodate all the pupils by 1674. The map provides evidence of the Corporation's own building programme. As early as December 1667 Samuel Pepys noted how quickly Guildhall was being rebuilt; by 1671 the Old Bailey Sessions House had been completed, the Wood Street Compter was more or less finished, and Newgate Prison was well under way. The Monument (it appears on the map as 'The Pillar where yᵉ fire began 1666') was completed in 1675.

Two large projects included in the Rebuilding Acts and shown on the Ogilby and Morgan map ended in failure. The first is the Thames Quay, intended to provide London with a river frontage to rival that of Continental cities. Much of the river frontage on the map is shown cleared of buildings, and on sheets 19 and 20 we see the 'New Key.' This, in the opinion of the City Surveyor and planning historian, Sydney Perks, is what in law was supposed to exist, not what actually existed. T. F. Reddaway, the historian of the Great

Fire, on the other hand, was inclined to think the map correct in parts but not in all. The second large civic project was the improvement of the Fleet River, an ambitious attempt at turning a nuisance into a benefit. It was dredged, made navigable to Holborn Bridge, and flanked by thirty foot wharves with underground storehouses.Unfortunately the 'Canal', as it was called at this time, was not used enough to justify the cost of its upkeep, and gradually it reverted to its former state.

The removal of the worst features of the old City made it a more attractive place to live in. The aldermen were supposed to reside in the City, and although this rule was relaxed after the Fire, it was again in force with few exceptions in 1675. Of the thirty-six great mansions named in Morgan's index, fourteen were of the houses of City aldermen. The houses of four of the five aldermen on the survey's vetting committee are depicted and supplied with map references.

*The reliability of the City survey**

How reliable is the topographical detail on Ogilby and Morgan's map? According to Gregory King, the map as begun by Leybourn 'particularized nothing'; it was he, Gregory King, who 'formed a New Project of that Survey at 100 feet per Inch', thus making it possible for the ground plot of every house and garden to be expressed. In their report to the Court of Aldermen, the vetting committee stated that not only 'Publick Buildings', but 'indeed every single House' had been measured. Leybourn and Holwell in their surveying manuals both imply that every house would have been surveyed. Leybourn, however, when listing the various classes of buildings surveyed for Ogilby's map, makes no specific mention of private houses.

To discover whether they were consistently and accurately shown it is revealing to compare sample areas of Ogilby and Morgan's map with manuscript surveys carried out in roughly the same period. The three described below have been selected on account of their large scale, the high reputation of the surveyors employed, and the fact that the clients' needs were such that the detail had to be accurate.

(i) 'Planographie or Ground-plot, of Severall Messuages or Tenements & Yards & Back-sides in Little Britain, and in a Court there called ... Pilkington Place ...' carried out for Christ's Hospital by William Leybourn, 1676. (Deposited at Guildhall Library – La Pr 352/LIT(1)). Comparing the appropriate area on sheet 12 of Ogilby and Morgan with this plan one discovers that one or two buildings that indisputably existed are not shown on Ogilby's. Ground plans of buildings often conform. Discrepancies, however, occur particularly

at the backs of buildings. The workhouse by St Bartholomew's new churchyard, shown on the Christ's Hospital plan as a single block, is shown on Ogilby's as a row of houses.

(ii) 'An exact survey of the Hospital and Precint of St. Catherine's near the Tower of London ...' carried out for the Master of St Katherine's Hospital by Gregory King and Edward Bostock Fuller, 1687. (Deposited at Guildhall Library – Map case 290). Comparing the area to the east of the Tower on sheet 20 of Ogilby and Morgan's map with the area to the west on this plan one discovers that some parts of the map are virtually identical. Rather more buildings, alleys, and courtyards, however, are shown in other parts of the St Katherine's map, and the pattern of buildings behind the streets is generally more complex.

(iii) Plan of the house of Judge Jeffreys, Aldermanbury, carried out for the City Lands Committee by John Olley, *c.*1701. According to the deed, Jeffrey's house was newly constructed in 1672. The courtyard on the Aldermanbury front of the mansion appears much the same on both plans. Yards and stables shown at the back of the building in the manuscript plan, however, do not appear on Ogilby and Morgan's map.

The most obvious conclusions to draw from careful study of such samples are these. The number of buildings shown in the main streets on the Ogilby and Morgan map is likely to be correct. The outline ground plans of these buildings may also be correct. The information supplied in alleys and courts is less dependable and in some cases diagramatic. Ogilby and Morgan's City of London map, the user must always bear in mind, is not a large-scale Ordnance Survey plan, and it should not be used as if it were.

Subsequent ventures

Following Ogilby's death, his successor, William Morgan, valiantly tried to keep the over-ambitious *English Atlas* project going. On 5 April 1677 the aldermen were faced with a new petition from him, asking for compensation for having compiled the City survey. Three years later they responded with a grant of £50.0s.0d. To bring in extra revenue lotteries were organised, Ogilby's books and copies of the City of London survey serving as prizes. The first of these was held at Jonathan's Coffee House in Sweeting Alley on 1 May 1677. Some support came from Livery Companies but it was disappointingly slight. The Fishmongers' curtly instructed their Clerk to order Morgan 'to take down his greate Mapp of London by him hanged up in the Hall This Court considering That at present they have noe use thereof nor any convenient place for the placing thereof.'

During Ogilby's lifetime, Gregory King and Robert Felgate had surveyed Westminster on the

same scale as the City map. A draft of this map was presented by Morgan to the King, and a survey of Southwark was put in hand. Instead of engraving these in the same manner as the City map, however, Morgan, on good advice, and no doubt in the interests of economy, reduced the three surveys to a single map on a scale of $c.17\frac{1}{2}$ inches to the mile. The map, entitled 'London &c. Actually Survey'd', measured $44\frac{1}{4} \times 93$ inches (1124 x 2362 mm.) Its publication was announced in the *London Gazette*, 19-23 January 1682. The many elaborate 'ornaments' on this map included the image of John Ogilby handing the subscription book for the 'Britannia' series to King Charles II (see frontispiece).

The other venture related to Ogilby's survey of the City was the Description. As we have seen, the material for it was already being assembled in 1673, the Court of Aldermen's vetting committee in that year expressing satisfaction with its progress. Robert Hooke was involved in June 1674, to the extent of writing an application to Guildhall on Ogilby's behalf asking for access to the City's records. The application was favourably considered on 9 July. The Chamberlain, the Common Sergeant, the Town Clerk, the four attorneys in the Outer Court (i.e. the Mayor's Court), and the surveyors of new buildings, were all instructed to draw up 'such remarks and memorials touching the ancient or present state of the City that they shall think fit to be inserted in the historical and geographical part of the Survey ... and present them to this Court.' An interesting feature of the Description was that it was to be illustrated by ward maps. These were being completed in 1676. After Ogilby's death and the publication of the 20-sheet City of London map, Morgan seems to have paid little attention to the Description. When Richard Blome took over various parts of the 'Britannia' project, publication of the Description, however, was considered again. Indeed the projected volume was advertised by Blome in the *London Gazette* on 23-27 January 1695. The text substantially expanded and updated, finally seems to have seen the light of day in 1720, in the form of John Strype's two-volumed *Survey of London*. Leybourn and Blome receive acknowlement in it wherever appropriate. The illustrations include what surely must be the Ogilby and Morgan ward maps, Blome's details erased from their cartouches.

† This essay represents a reduced version of the text that accompanies the facsimile of Ogilby and Morgan's map of the City of London, published in 1976 by Harry Margary in association with Guildhall Library. The sources used are to be found in the same publication. The author wishes in particular to thank James Sewell, City Archivist at the Corporation of London Record Office for his valuable assistance.

* For other researchers' opinions on the reliability of the Ogilby and Morgan survey, see Herbert Berry, *The Boar's Head Playhouse* (Washington DC: Folger Books 1986), appendix 7, 'The Accuracy of Ogilby and Morgan's Map'; and *The British Atlas of Historic Towns ... The City of London from Prehistoric Times to c.1520* (Oxford: O.U.P. 1989), chapter VII – 'Introduction to the Maps', by Henry Johns.

PUBLISHER'S NOTE

Each pair of pages in this volume is a full-scale reproduction of half a sheet of the original Ogilby and Morgan map.

The publisher thanks the Corporation of London's Greater London Record Office for allowing their copy of Ogilby and Morgan – the most perfectly preserved copy known – to be reproduced for the present publication. Peter Jackson, Chairman of the London Topographical Society, is thanked for drawing the key map.

FURTHER READING

BARKER, Felix, and JACKSON, Peter, *The History of London in Maps* (London: Barrie & Jenkins 1990)

EERDE, Katherine van, *John Ogilby and the Taste of his Times* (Folkestone: Dawson 1976)

GLANVILLE, Philippa, *London in Maps* (London: 'Connoisseur' 1972)

HARLEY, J.B., Intrductory notes to the facsimile publication, *John Ogilby: Britannia, London, 1675* (Amsterdam: T.O.T. 1970)

HIND, Arthur M., *Wenceslaus Hollar and his Views of London and Windsor in the Seventeenth Century* (London: John Lane the Bodley Head 1922)

HOWGEGO, James J., *Printed Maps of London, c.1553-1850*, 2nd edn. (Folkestone: Dawson 1978)

HYDE, Ralph, Introductory notes to the facsimile publication, *A Large and Accurate Map of the City of London, by John Ogilby and William Morgan, 1676* (Lympne: Harry Margary in association with Guildhall Library 1976)

HYDE, Ralph, Introductory notes to the facsimile publication, *London &c. Actually Survey'd, 1682* (Lympne: Harry Margary in association with Guildhall Library 1977)

SCHUCHARD, Margaret, *John Ogilby, 1600-1676: Lebensbild eines Gentleman mit vielen Karrieren* (Hamberg: Paul Hartung 1973)

SKELTON, R.A., *County Atlases of the British Isles, 1579-1703* (London: Carta Press 1970)

TYACKE, Sarah, *London Map-Sellers* (Tring, Herts.: Map Collector Publications 1978)

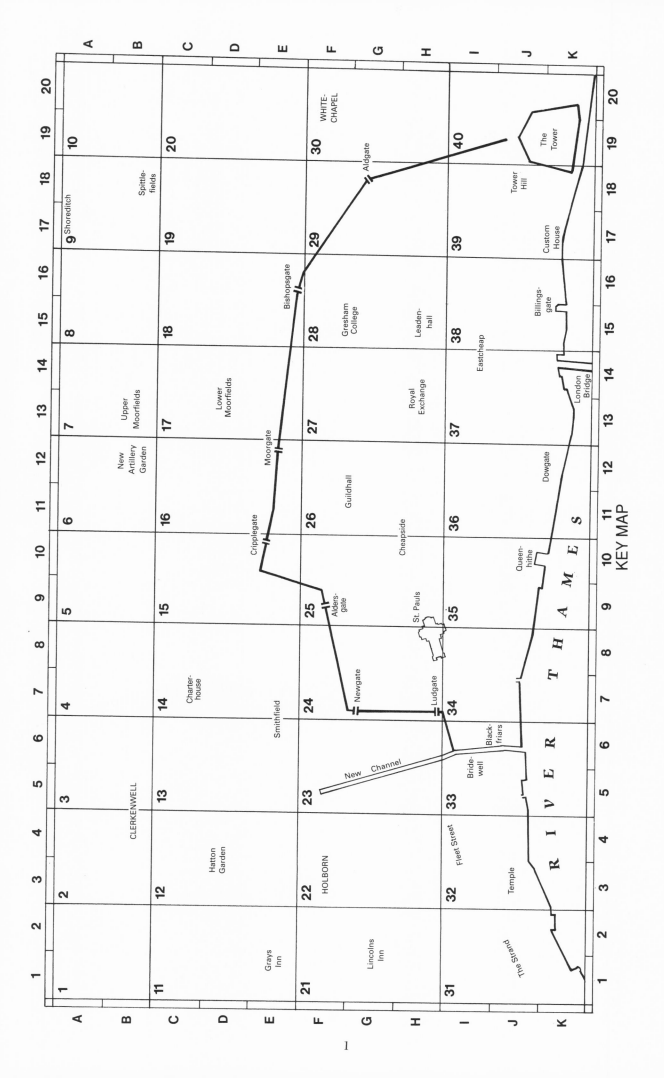

KEY MAP

1

A L A

A

E

G

R

Ichnographically Defcribing

Garden

Garden

Garden

Garden

Garden

Garden

Garden

Garden

Garden

Pond

New Corporation Court Yard.

Bride well

A Church Yard for Garden

Bowling Green

Bowling Green

Bowling Green

Bowling

Pasture

Duck-Pond

a2

3

4

A

A

A

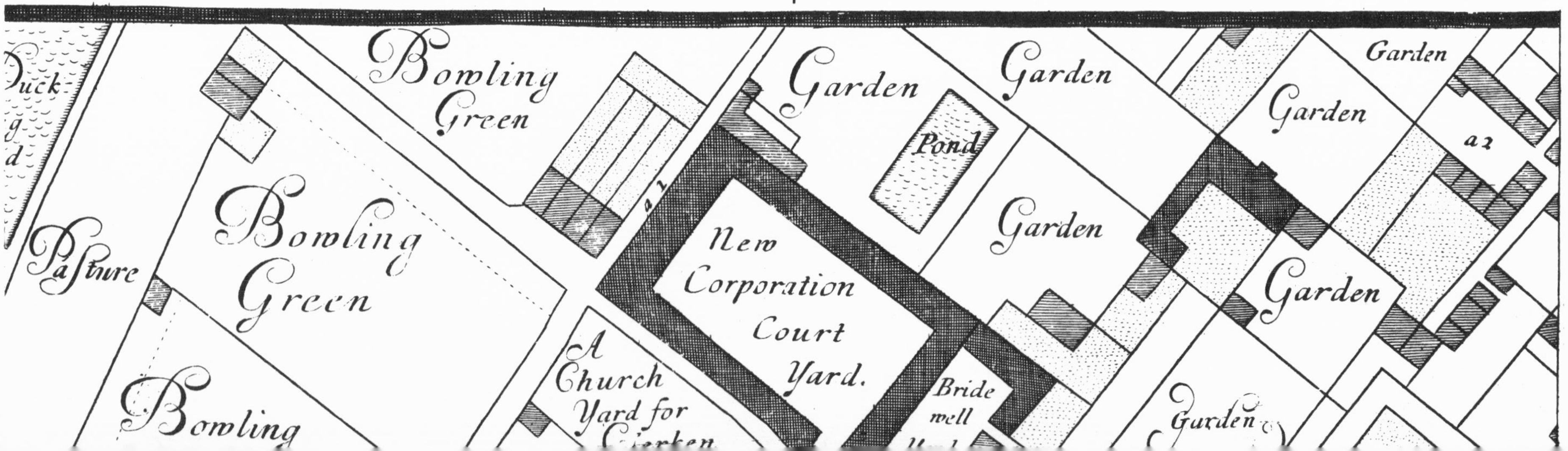

A N D C

all the Streets, Lanes,

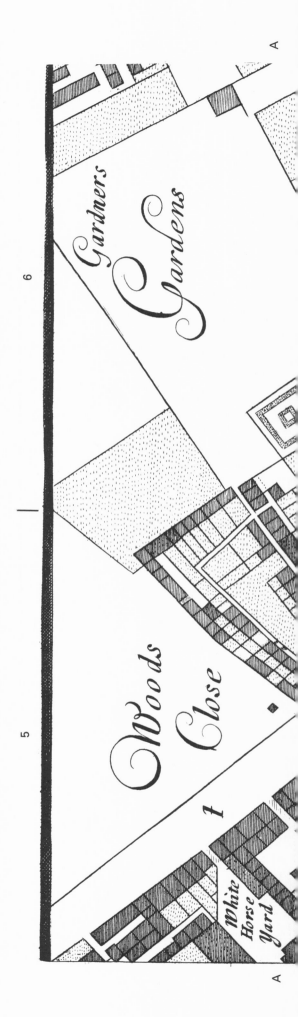

C U R A

Alleys, Courts, Yards,

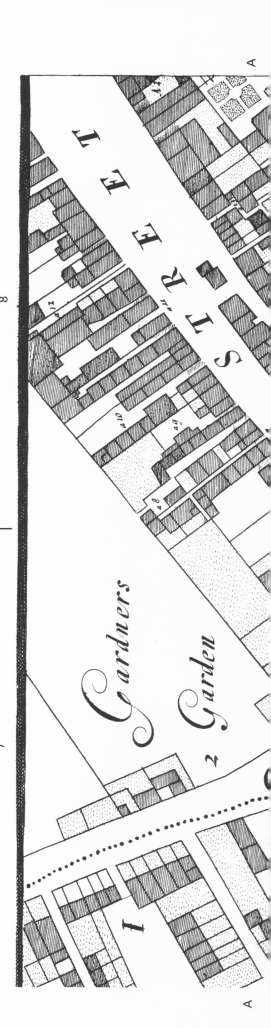

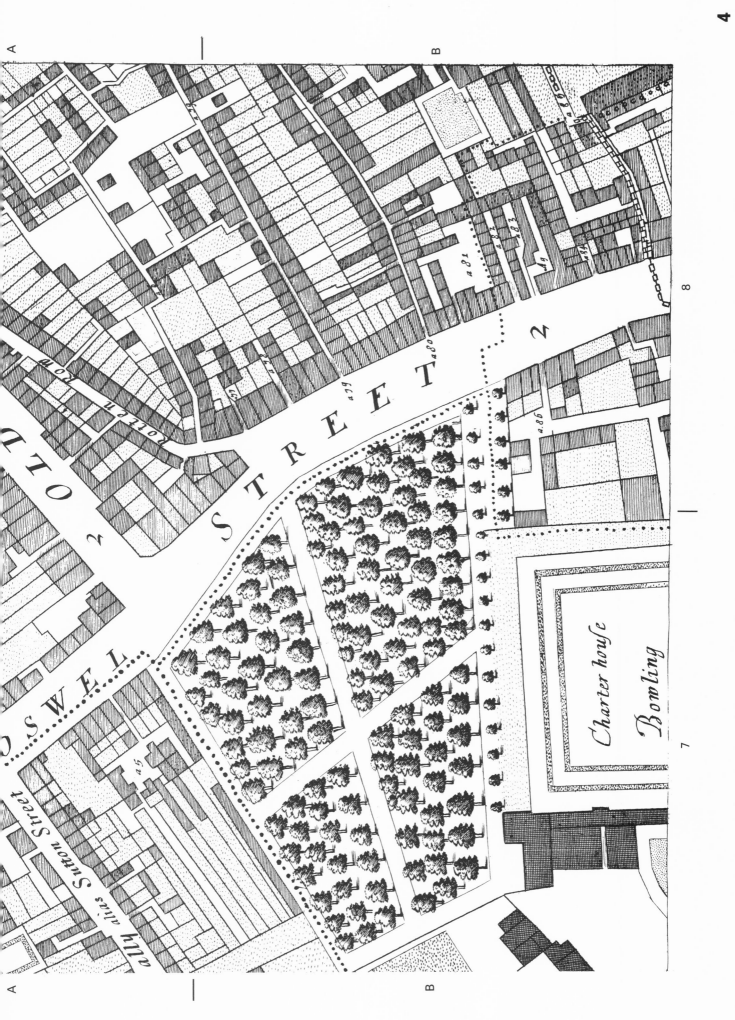

T E M

Churches, Halls and Houſ

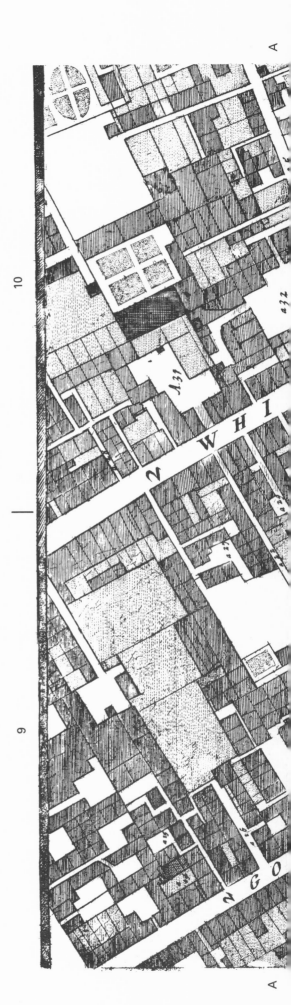

A P P O F

es, &c. Actually Surveyed

Church Yard

2

2

12

11

12

A A

A

The New Artillery Garden

BUN HILL

A Dye house Yard

T H E C

and Delineated, By

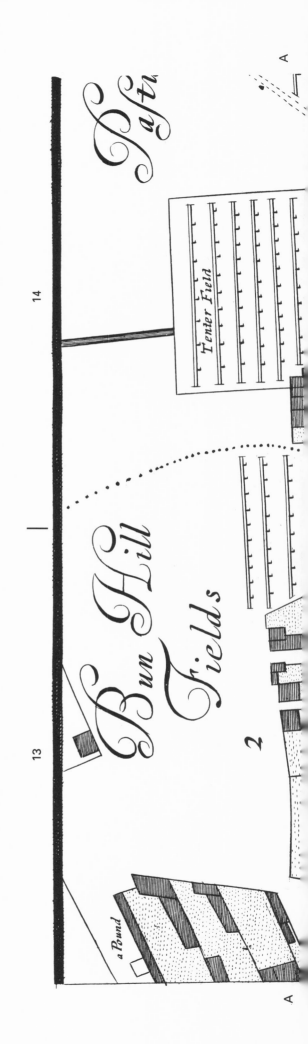

a Pound

Bun Hill Fields

Tenter Field

Pastu

13   14

2

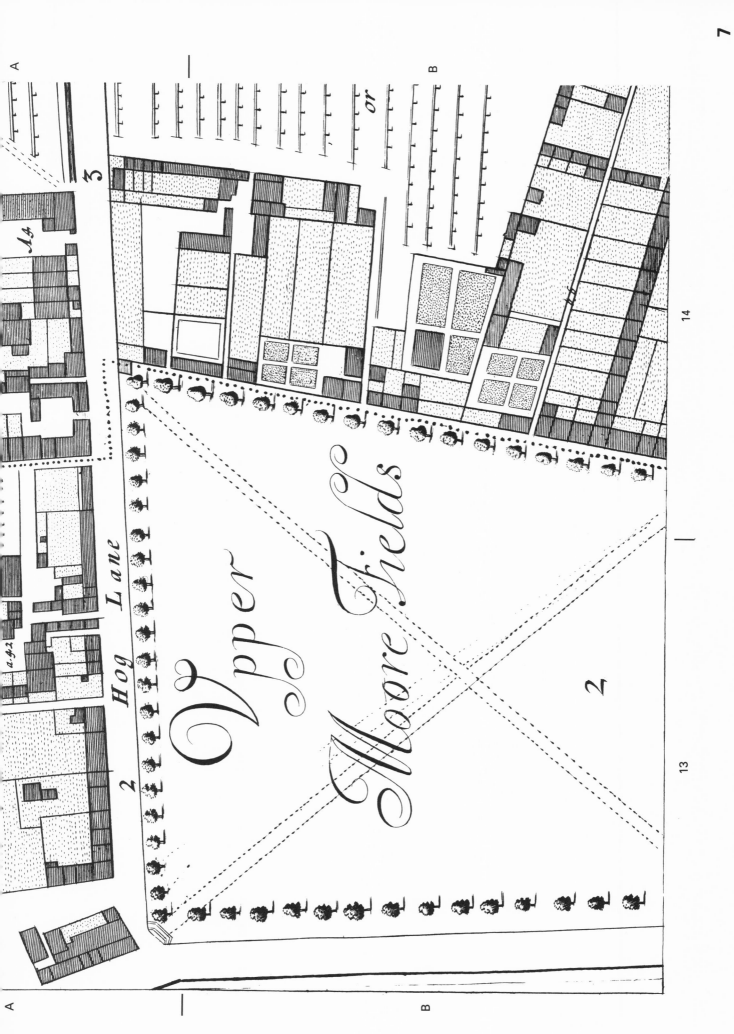

I T Y O

JOHN OGILBY, Efq; His

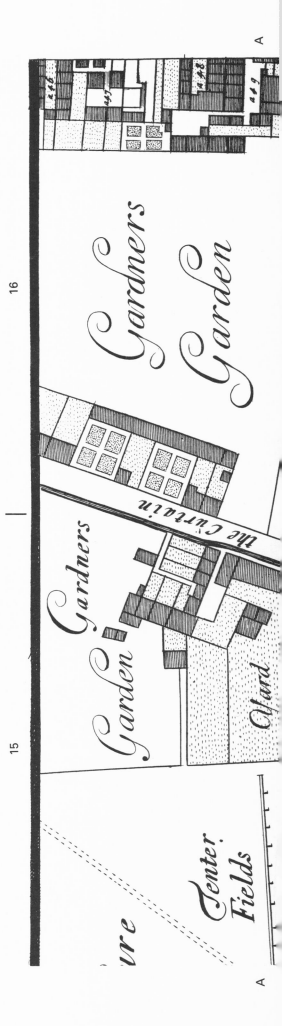

NORTHERN FOLGATE

HOG LANE

the Hovil

Butchers Close

Tenter Field

Yarden

F L O

Majesties Cosmographer.

20

19

A

B

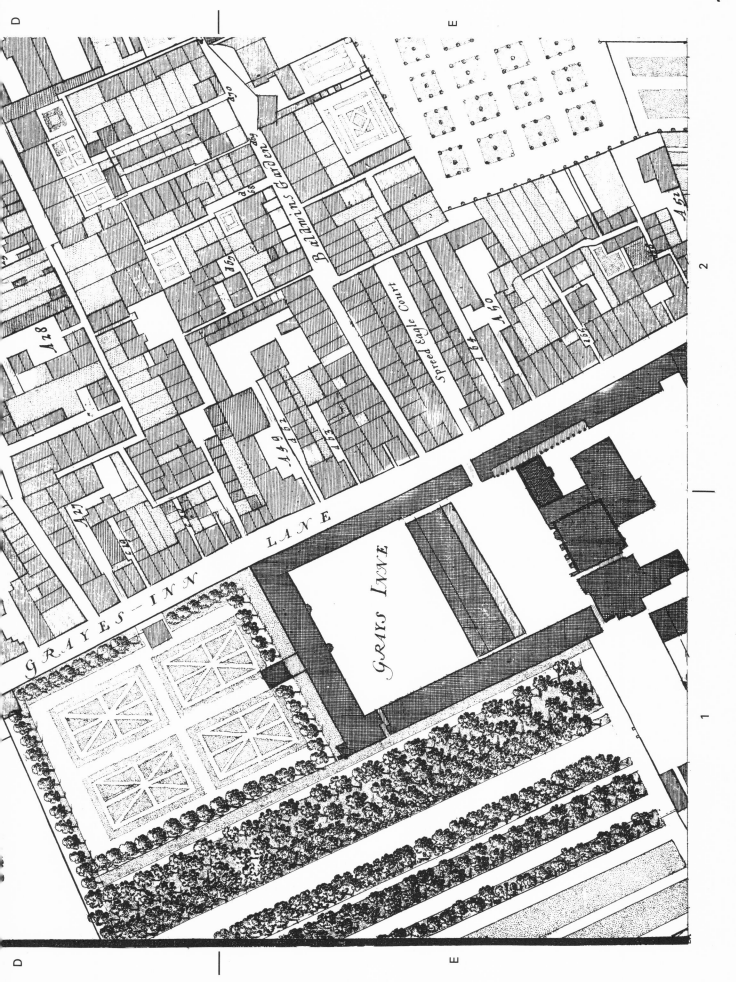

13

26

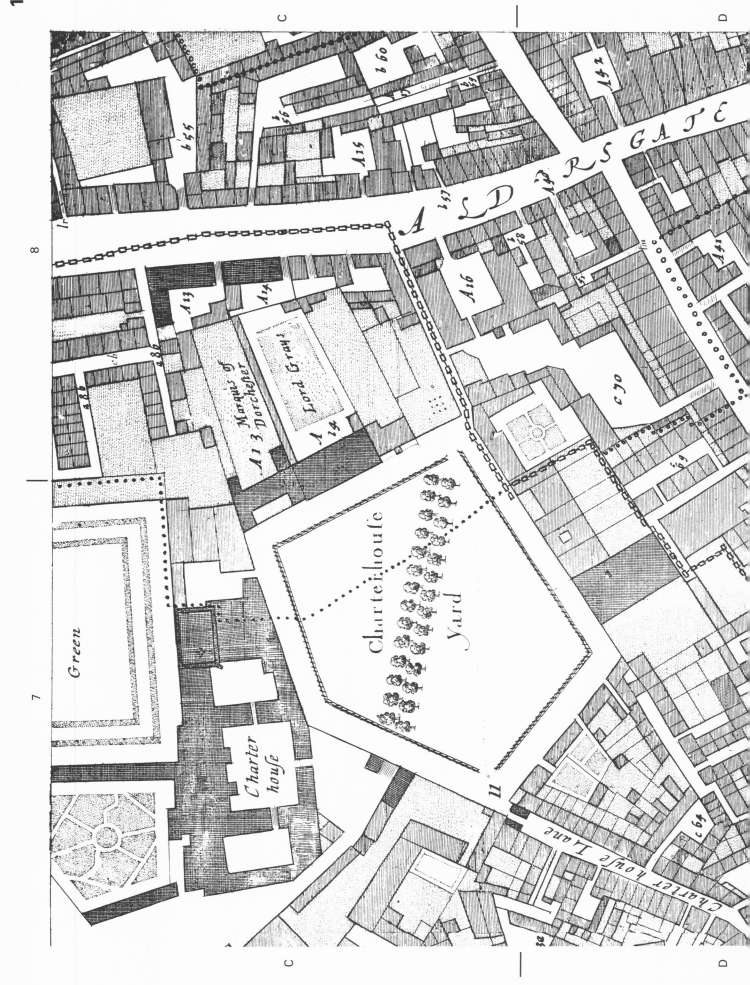

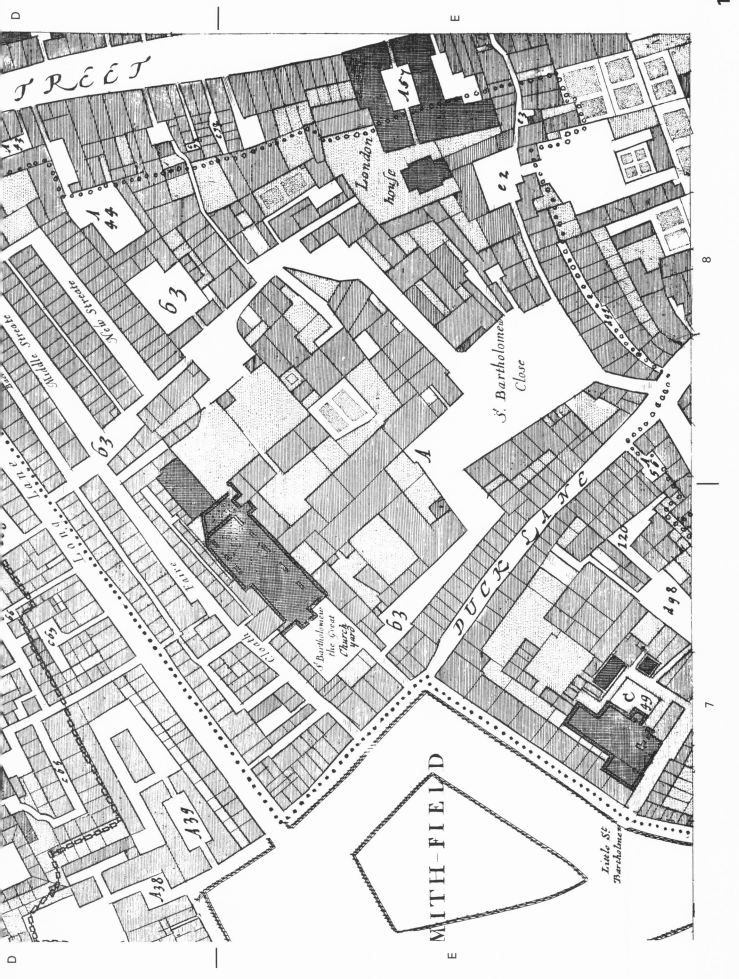

TREET

D
D

44

63

New Streate

Middle Streate

Lane

Long

Cloath Faire

Cloath

438

439

163

MITH-FIELD

E

St Bartholomew the Great Church yard

63

St Bartholomew Close

London house

467

62

63

DUCK LANE

A

120

498

C
49

Litle St: Bartholmew

E

8

7

Chiſwell Street

Chiſwell Street

12

11

A . 22

A . 22

A . 22

A·23

C

C

D

D

Q

b.87

b.90

b.93

b.94

b.96

c.97

b.89

b.91

b.92

b.78

b.79

Fields

b.99

b.19

b.20

Sugar loaſe Court

Rams head Court

Grub Street

LANE

L

c.96

c.98

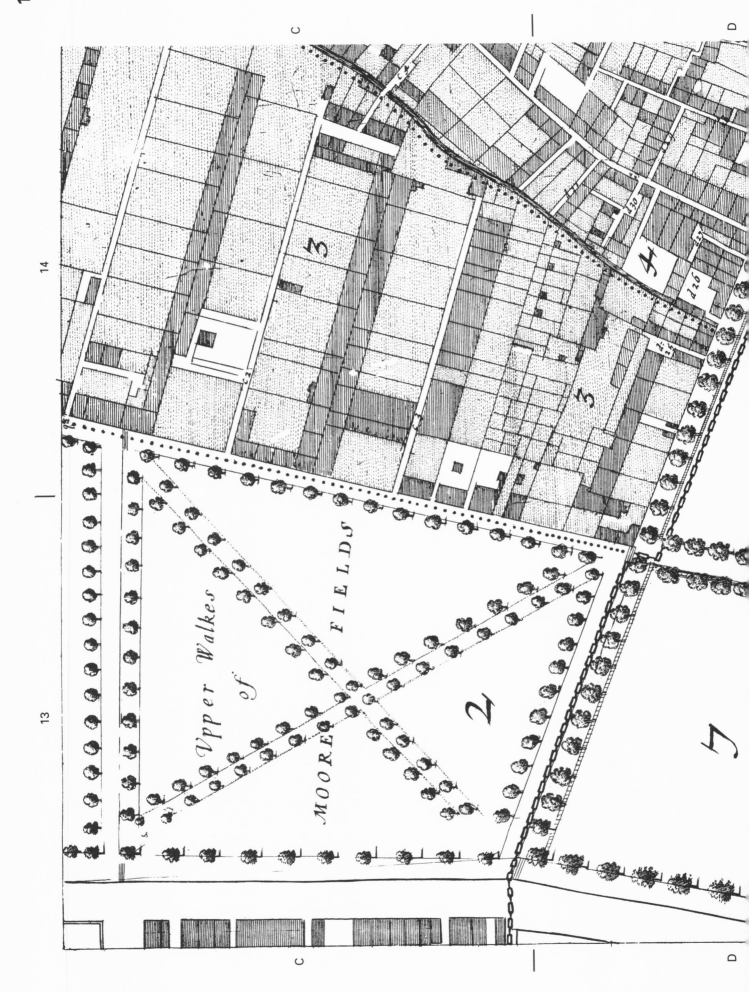

D D

A48

449

Vine Court

Hand

DC

H

GA

5

473

260

5

262

A74

HOUNS DITCH

BISHOPS GATE

438

439

461

440

P

262

475

Bishops Gate

BETHELEM

P

259

S. Buttolphs with out Bishopgate

16

Bishops

5

460

P2

254

PETTY France

CHURCH YARD

K

P

Wormwood Street

256

15

HILEHEM

HURCH

R B

D

E E

37

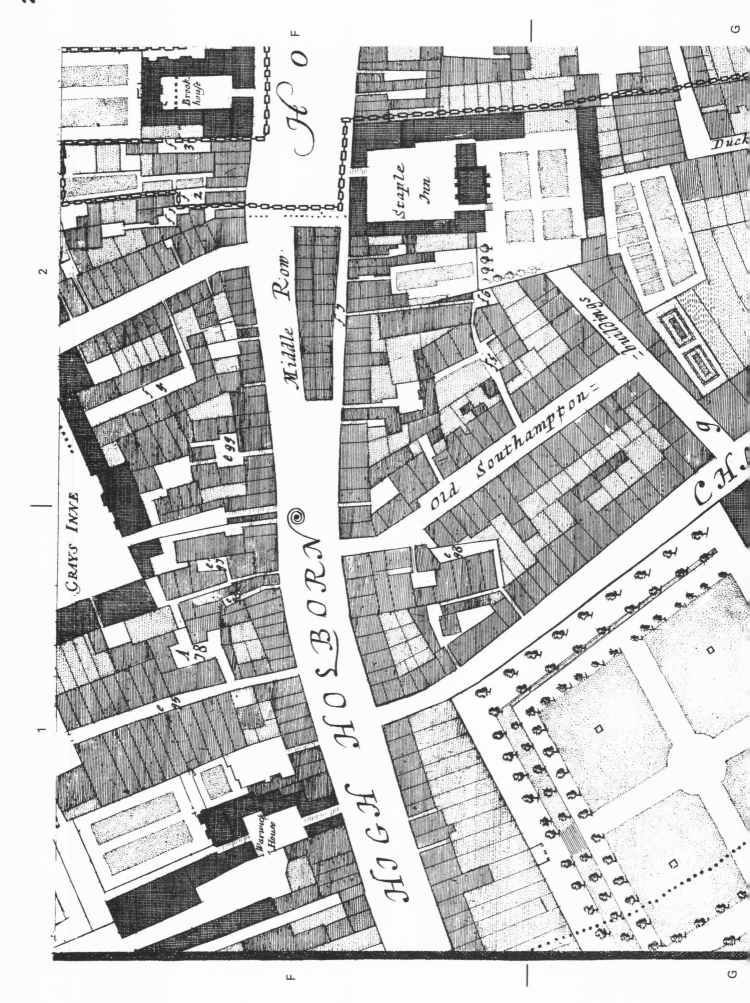

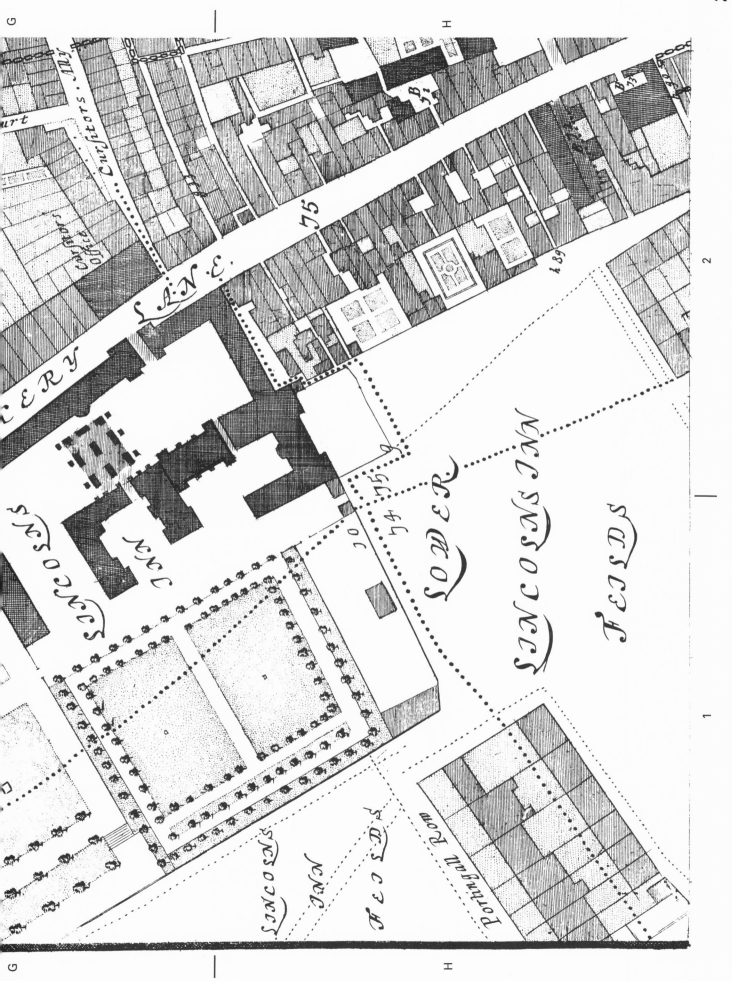

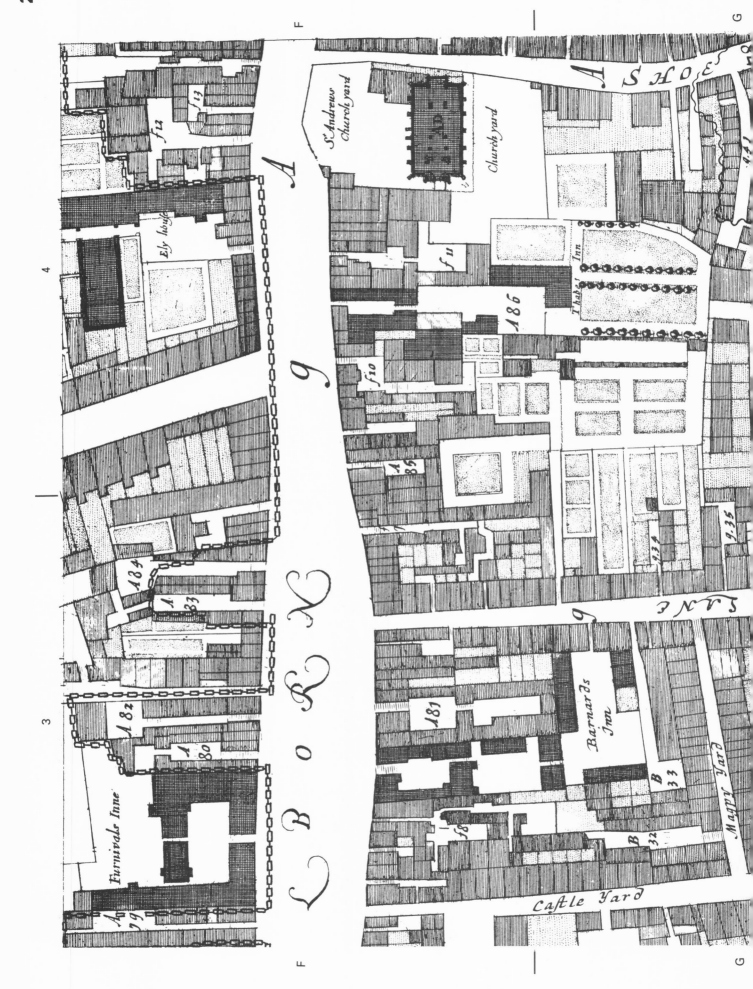

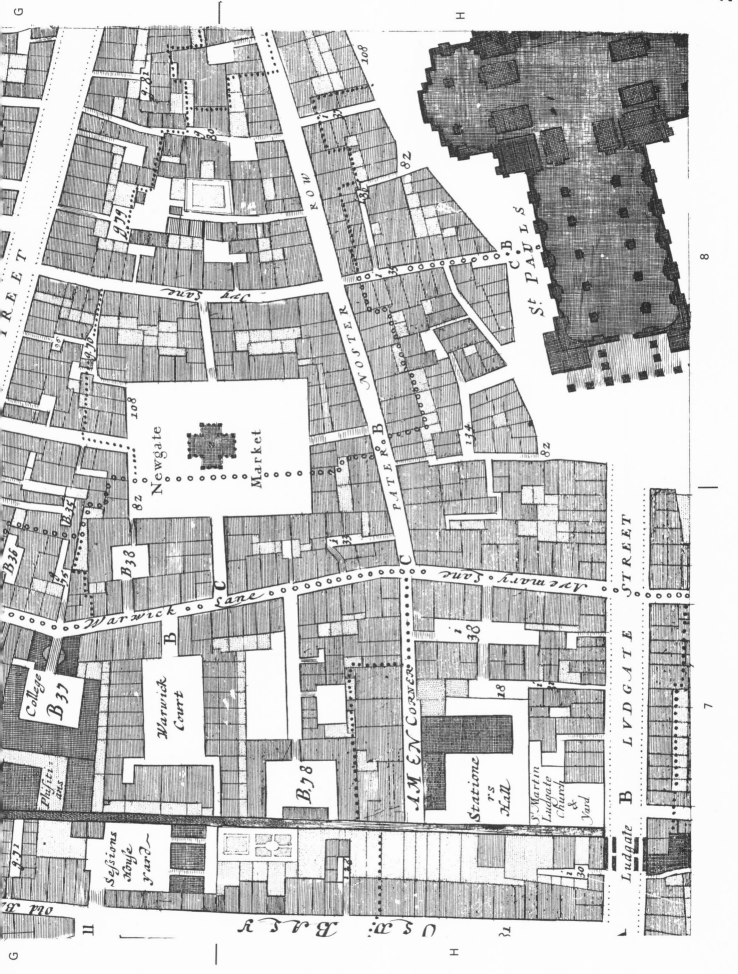

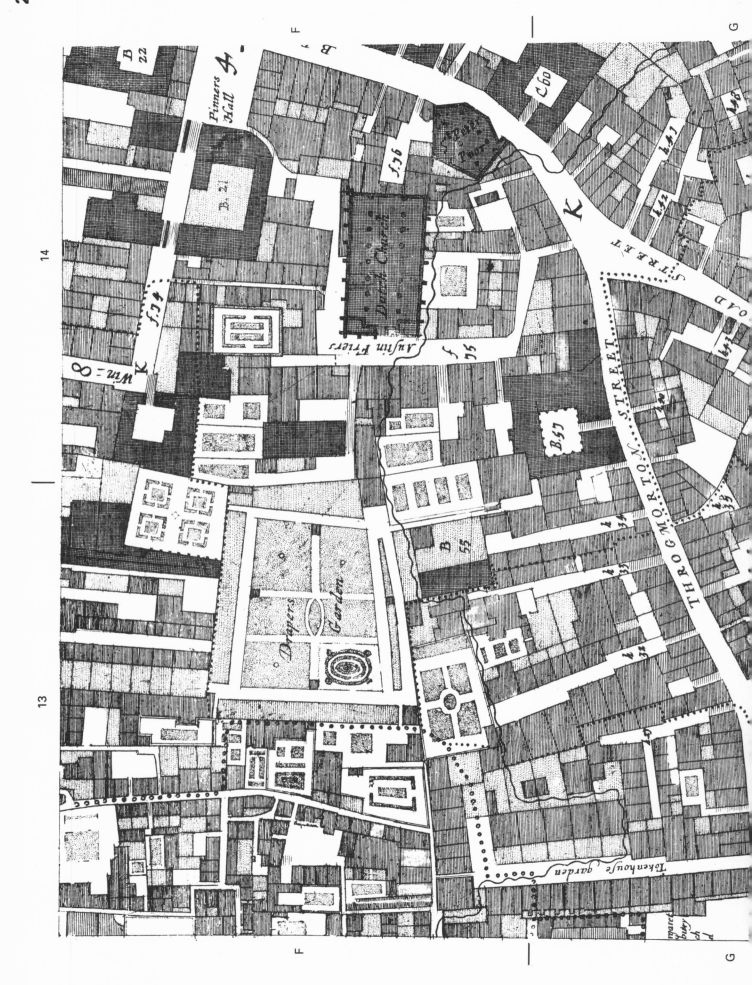

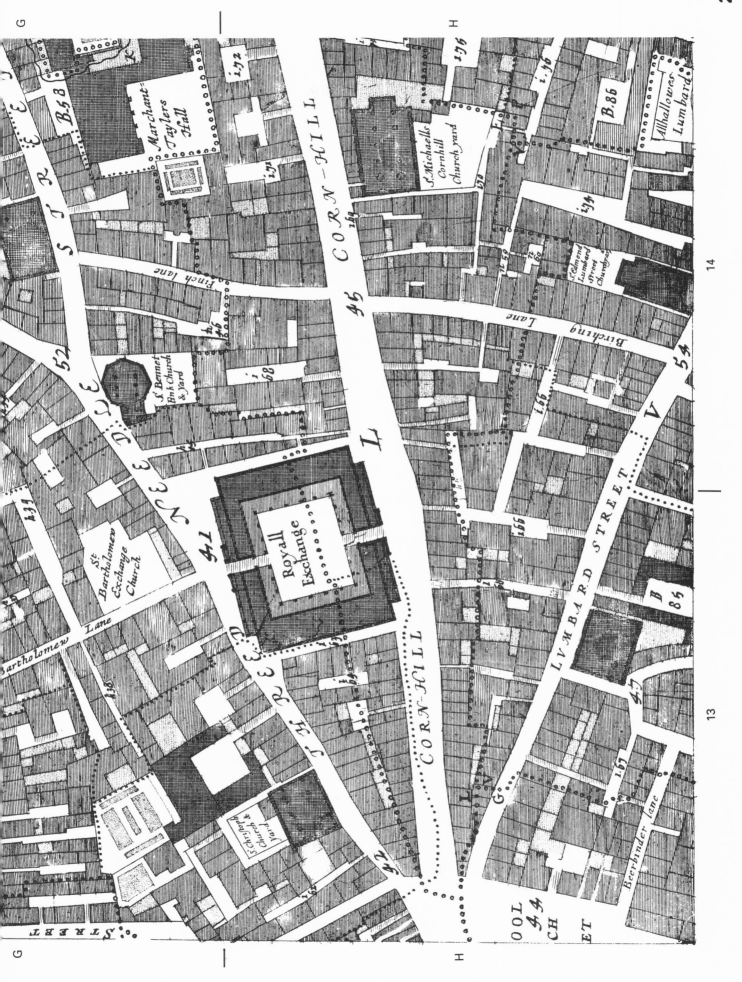

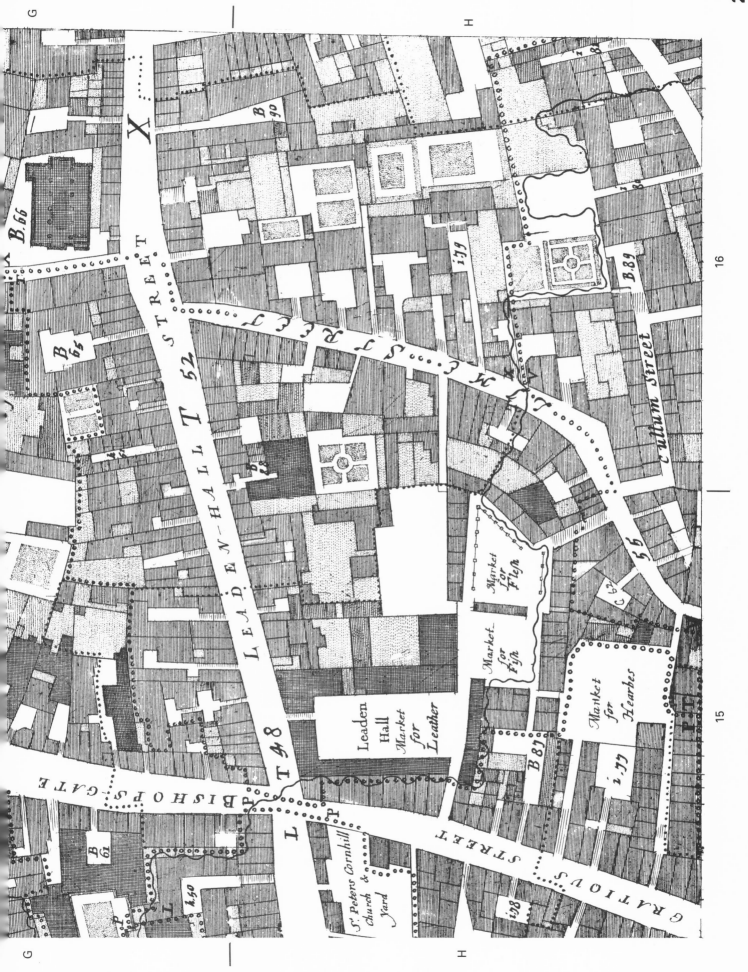

G

G

B.66

B.65

B.69

1.50

X

STREET

LEADEN-HALL STREET

T 52

T 48

BISHOPS-GATE

P P

L P

L

St Peters Cornhill church & Yard

B.83

B.90

1.79

Market for Fish

Market for Fish

Leaden Hall Market for Leather

B.87

1.77

Market for Hearbes

C 62

B.89

Cullum street

55

GRATIOVS STREET

B.84

H

H

16

15

G G

B.93

B.92

CRUTCHED Friers 69

18

X

56

69.

B 59

59.

58

87

86

65.

C 54

C 53

Leaden-hall Street

Clock Yard

B 68

62.

17

FENCHURCH

St: Katherine Ch:
Coleman

85.

84.

83.

Butler Lane

B 96.

G G

H

H

G G

Goodmans

Fields

Trinity Minories
Church

THE MINORIES

W

H H

61

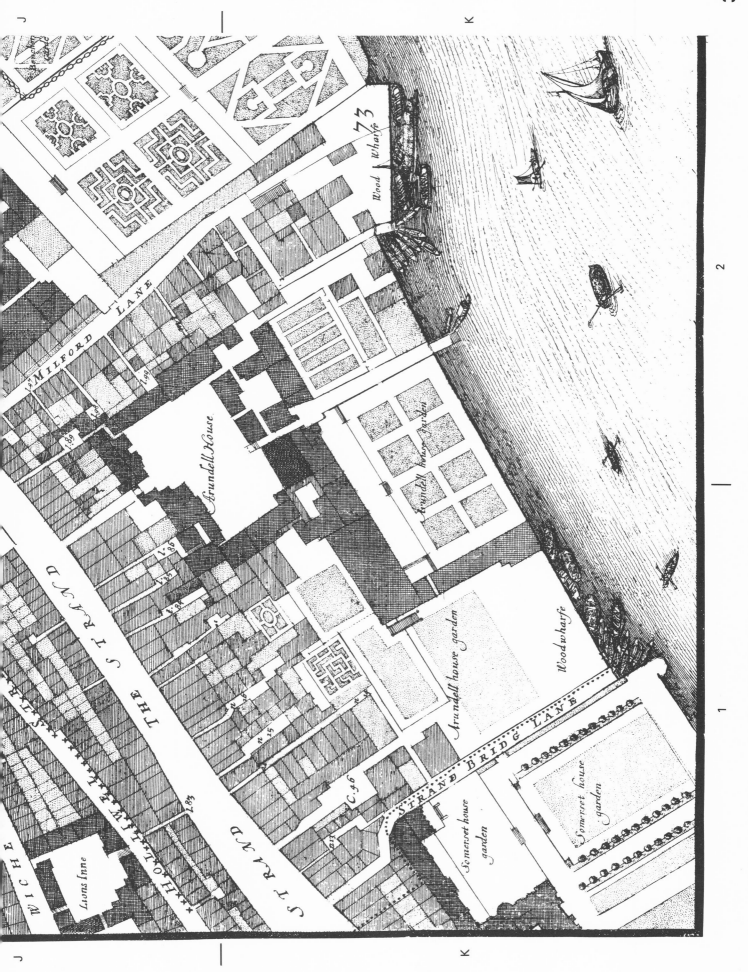

J

K

WICHE STREETE

Lions Inne

HOLLIWELL STREETE

THE STRAND

STRAND

283

285

C.36

n.15

MILFORD LANE

189

186

187

185

184

Arundell House.

190

191

Arundell house garden

Somerset house garden

STRAND BRIDG LANE

Arundell house garden

Somerset house garden

Woodwharfe

Wood wharfe

73

J

K

1

2

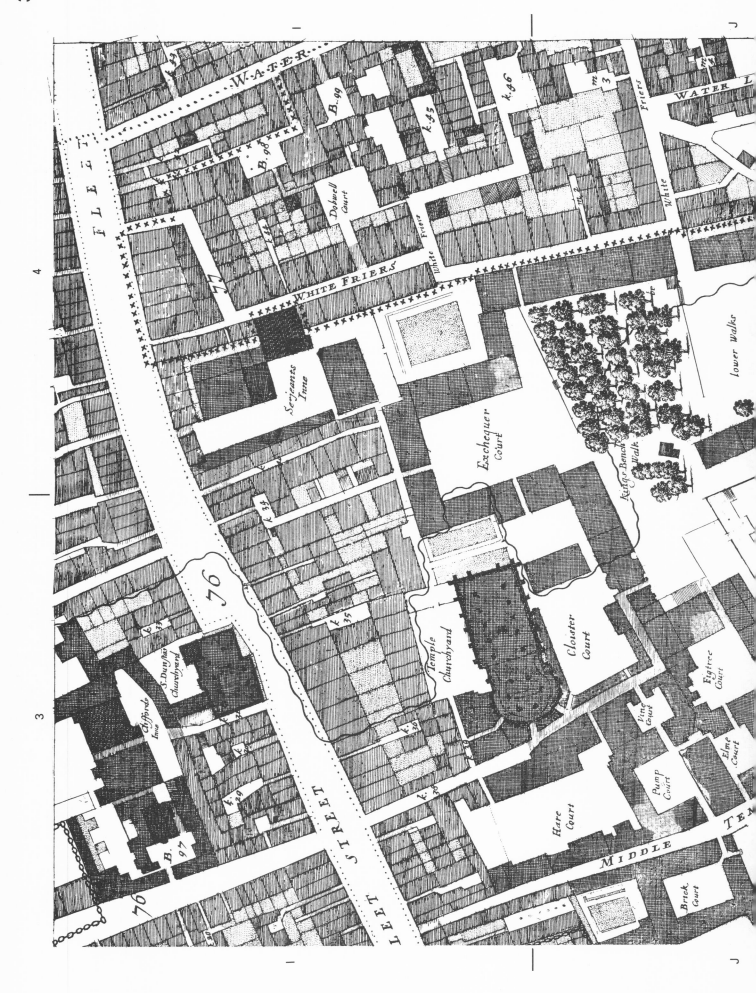

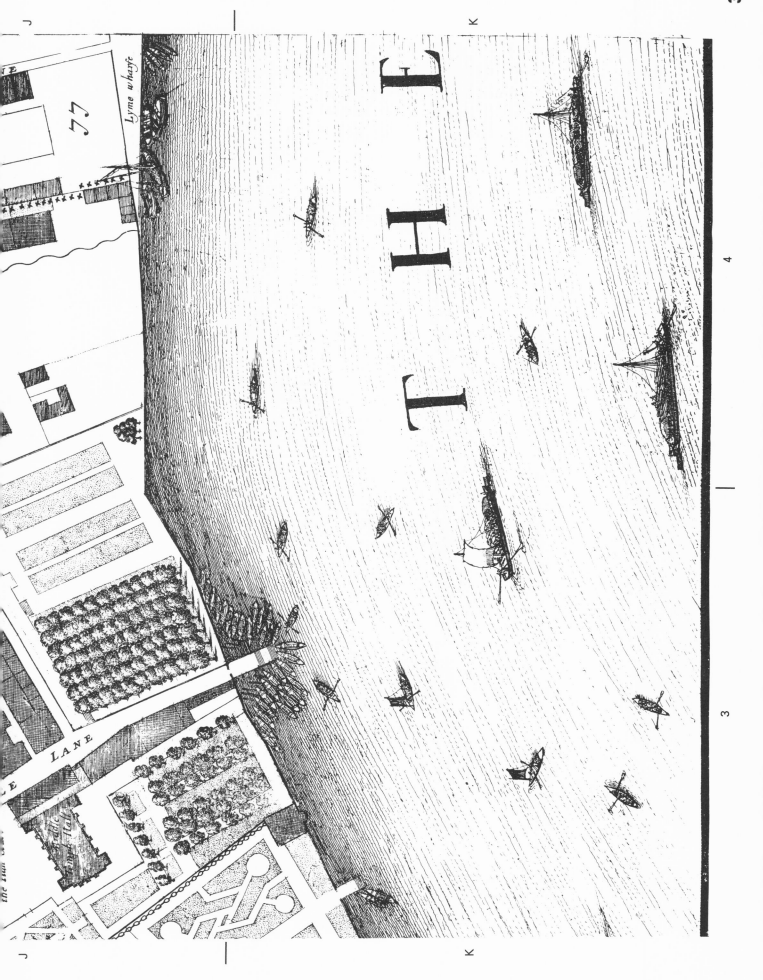

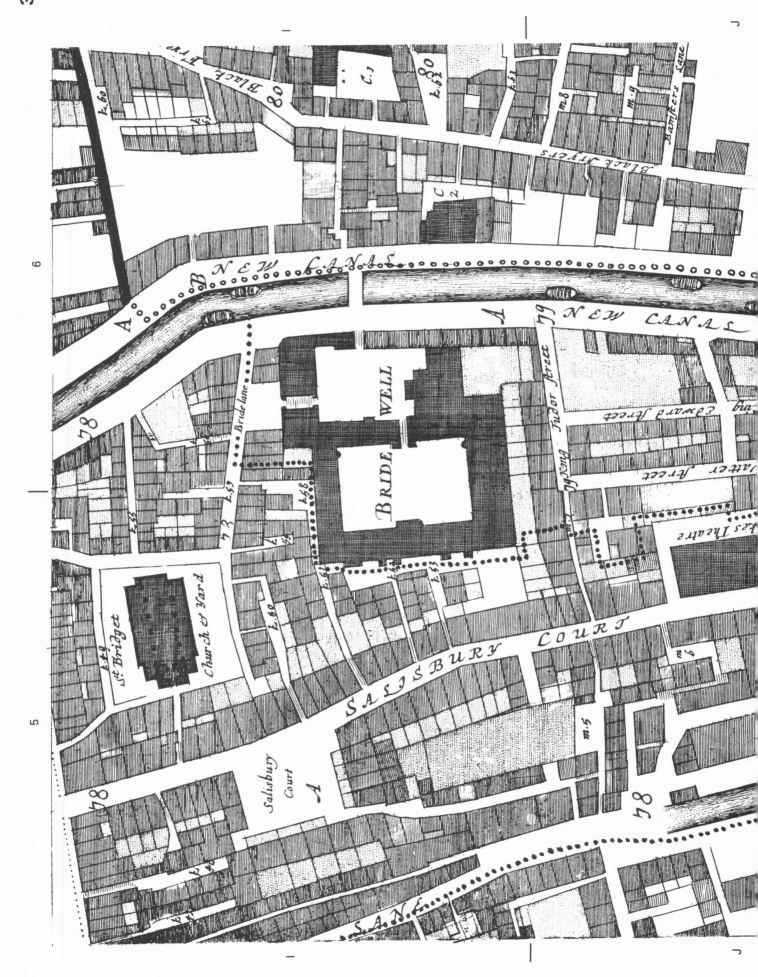

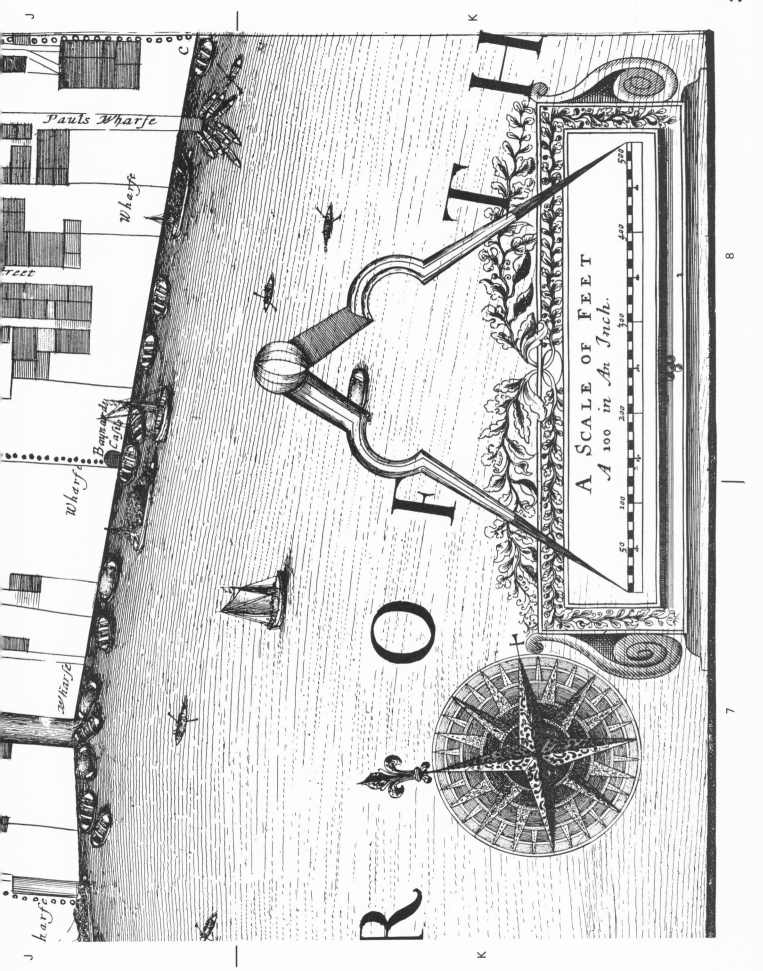

Pauls Wharfe

Wharfe

reet

Baynards Castle

Wharfe

wharfe

harfe

A SCALE OF FEET
A 100 in An Inch.

8

7

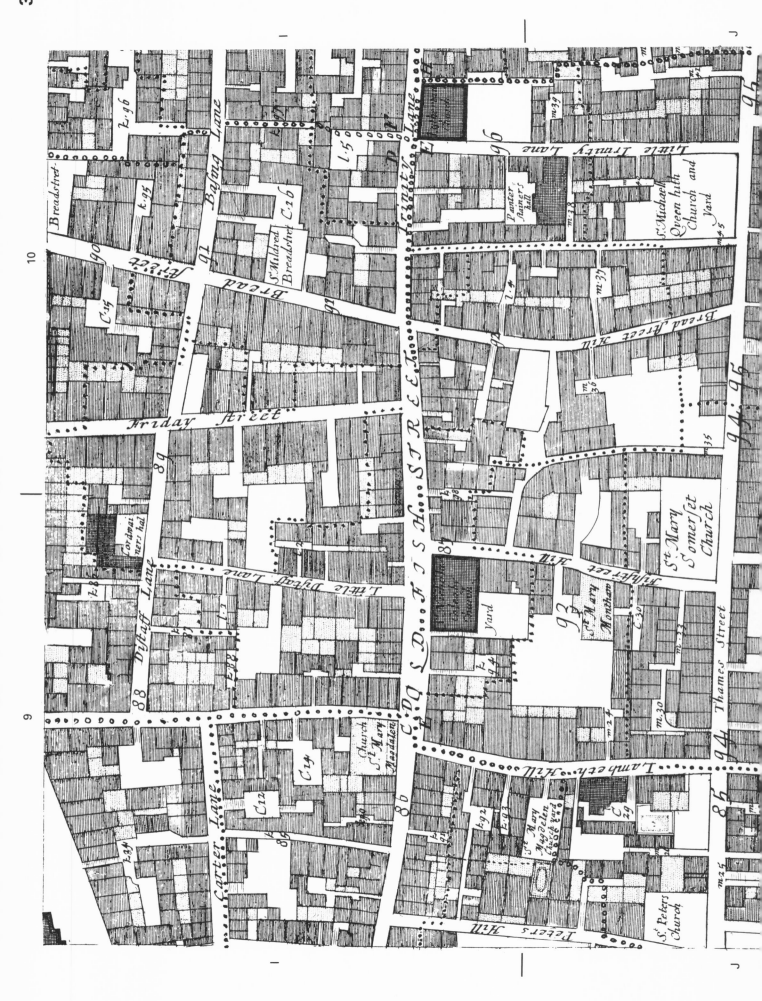

Towns End Lane

Queen Hith

Queen Hith Dock

m 43

Brookes Wharfe

Dunghill Lane

High Timber Street

Broken wharfe

31

Wood Wharfe

Trigg Lane

Wood wharfe

A   M   E   S

9   10

K   J

J   K

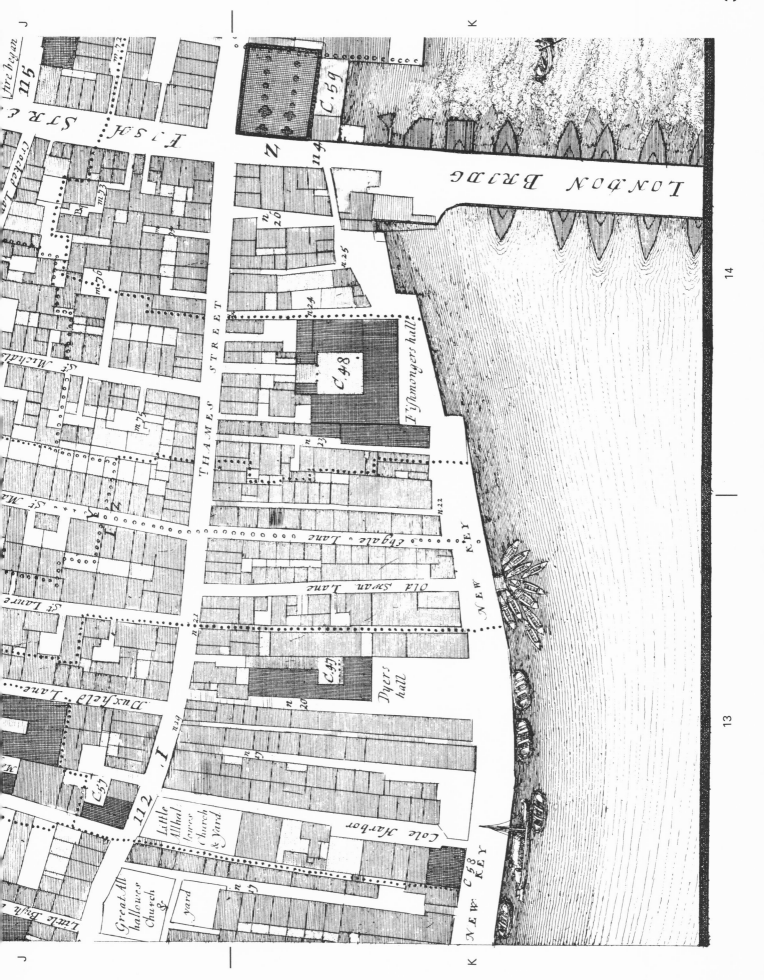

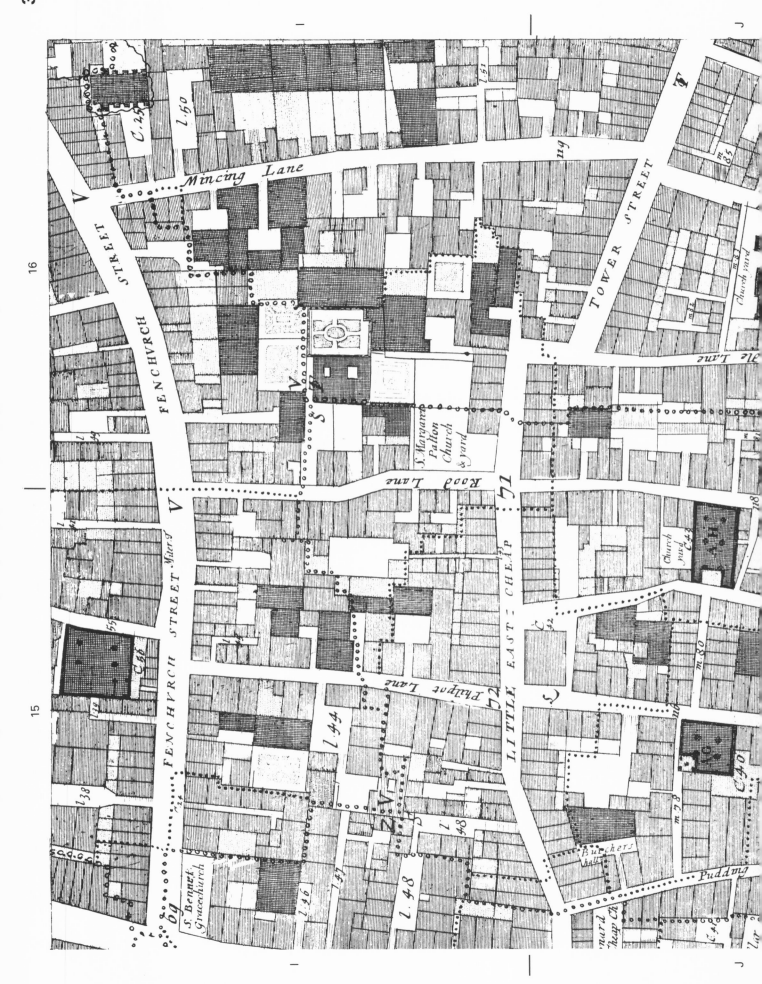

TOWER WHARFE

NEW KEY

Custome house

NEW KEY

STREET

THAMES

Beer Lane

Lane

Water

Church yard

REET

18

17

K

K

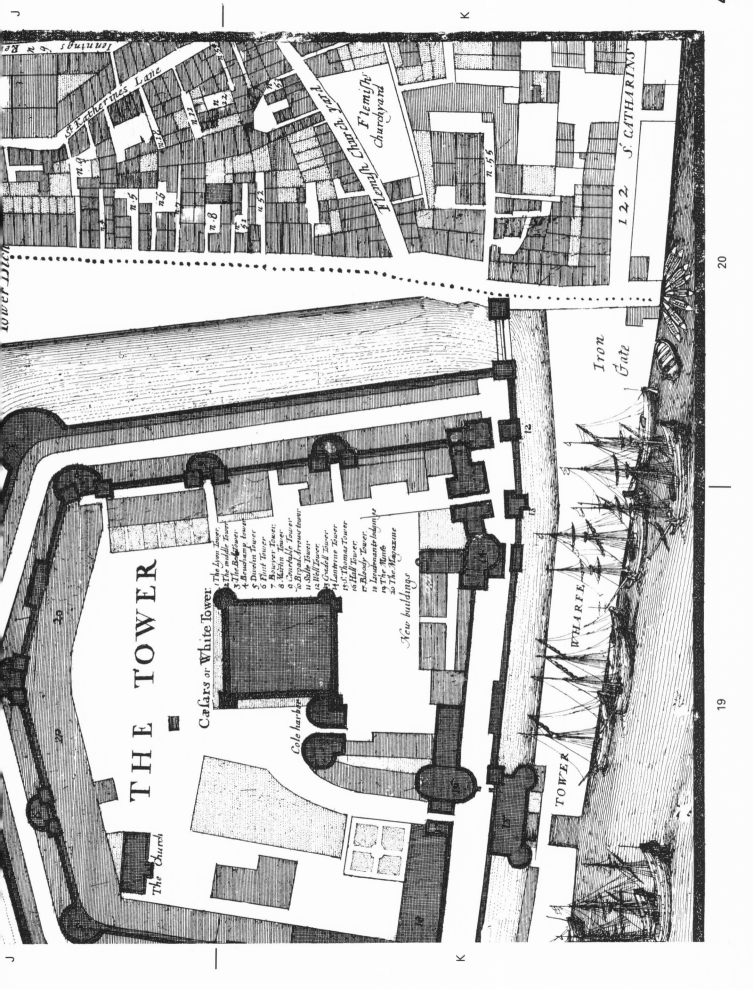

THE TOWER

Cæfars or White Tower.

The Church

Cole-har-br

1 The Lyon Tower.
2 The middle Tower.
3 The Bell Tower.
4 Beauchamp Tower.
5 Divelin Tower.
6 Flint Tower.
7 Bowyer Tower.
8 Martin Tower.
9 Conftable Tower.
10 Broad Arrow tower.
11 Salte Tower.
12 Well Tower.
13 Cradell Tower.
14 Lantorne Tower.
15 S. Thomas Tower.
16 Hall Tower.
17 Bloody Tower.
18 Lieutenants lodgings
19 The Mint.
20 The Magazine

New buildings

Flemish Church yard
Flemish Churchyard

St Katherines Lane

Jennings Rents

TOWER WHARFE

Iron Gate

St CATHARINS

122

PLACE NAME INDEX

This index is a simplified and corrected version of the *Explanation* which accompanies Ogilby and Morgan's Map of London, 1676. It contains entries for the great majority of streets, lanes, courts, alleys, etc., shown on the map, as well as churches, inns, halls of Livery Companies, residences of distinguished persons, and so forth. Streets and buildings listed in the *Explanation* but not named or numbered on the map have been omitted.

Streets and buildings are arranged in one alphabetical sequence. All places are entered under their first word, with the exception of names beginning with the definite article, and private buildings, which are entered under the surname of the occupier. Spelling has been brought up to date wherever possible; thus Lyon is spelled Lion, Key: Quay, Bore: Boar, Plow: Plough, etc.

Dolphin Inn (A95) - 23-F 6
Dolton's Yard (e63) - 19-E17
Dorchester, Marquess of, House of (A13) - 14-C 8
Dorset Street - 19-C18
Double Hood Court (m62) - 36-J12
Dove Court (i67) - 27-H13
Dove Court (i58) - 26-H12
Dowgate Dock Lane - 36-J12
Dowgate Hill - 36-J12
Draper's Court (h25) - 26-G12
Drapers' Hall (B57) - 27-G14
Duck Lane - 14-E 7
Duck's Court - 21-G 2
Duke's Place - 29-G17
Duke's Place Court - 29-G17
Dunghill Lane (m17) - 35-J10
Dunghill Lane (m17) - 34-J 7
Dunning's Alley (c13) - 18-C16
Dunstan's Alley (g67) - 28-G16
Dunstan's Court (h97) - 22-H 4
Dunstan's Court (150) - 40-J20
Dutch Church - 37-K13
Duxfield Lane - 37-J13
Dyer's Alley (f52) - 25-F 9
Dyer's Court (f63) - 26-F11
Dyers' Hall (C47) - 37-K13
Dyer's Yard (157) - 39-I17

Eagle and Child Alley (n8) - 40-J20
Eagle and Child Alley (g30) - 30-F20
Eagle and Child Alley (g49) - 23-G 5
Eagle Street - 10-A19
Eales's Yard (k3) - 30-H19
East Harding Street - 22-G 4
East India House (B88) - 28-H16
East Smithfield - 40-J20
Elbgate Lane - 37-K13
Elbow Lane - 36-J12
Ellis Court (g68) - 23-G 6
Elm Court - 32-J 3
Ely House - 32-F 4
Emperor's Head Lane (m58) - 36-J12
Essex Court - 31-J 2
Essex Court (k45) - 32-I 4
Essex House - 31-J 2
Exchange Alley (i66) - 27-H13
Exchequer Court - 32-J 4
Excise Office (C60) - 27-F14
Falcon Court (g44) - 22-G 4
Falcon Court (k35) - 32-J 3
Falconer's Alley (a89) - 5-B 9
Falcon Inn (B1) - 25-F 9
Falcon Inn (A28) - 11-D 2
Falcon Yard (f47) - 25-F 9
Fann's Alley (a85) - 4-B 8
Fashion Street - 20-C19
Feathers Alley (h89) - 21-H 2
Feathers Alley (f16) - 23-F 5
Feathers Court (h12) - 25-G10
Feathers Yard (d65) - 11-E 2

Fell Court (e22) - 27-G14
Fell Street - 27-G14
Fenchurch Alley (i80) - 28-H16
Fenchurch Street - 38-I15
Fenn Court (m77) - 37-J14
Fetter Lane - 22-G 3
Field Lane (f15) - 23-F 5
Fiery Pillar, The - 37-J14
Fig Tree Court (b63) - 15-C 9
Fig Tree Court - 13-D 5
Finch Lane - 27-G14
Finsbury Stables (A22) - 16-C12
Fire Ball Alley (g1) - 29-F17
Fire Ball Court (g2) - 29-F17
Fisher's Alley (f3) - 23-G 6
Fisher's Rents (g60) - 19-D17
Fishmongers' Hall (C48) - 31-K14
Fitchett's Court (f49) - 25-F 9
Five Foot Lane (m35) - 35-J10
Five Inkhorn Court (b91) - 16-C11
Fleece Alley (e97) - 21-F 1
Fleet Lane - 23-G 6
Fleet Street - 32-I 3
Flemish Church Yard - 40-K20
Flower de Luce Alley (h93) - 22-H 3
Flower de Luce Alley (c40) - 13-D 5
Flower de Luce Alley (m10) - 34-J 7
Flower de Luce Court, Foster Lane (g91) - 25-G10
Flower de Luce Court, Blackfriars (k76) - 20-D20
Flower de Luce Court, Grub St. (d1) - 27-H14
Flower de Luce Court, Houndsditch (f93) - 18-C16
Flower de Luce Court, Fleet St. (i20) - 29-G18
Flying Horse Court (k29) - 23-H 6
Flying Horse Court (a83) - 32-I 3
Flying Horse Court (d2) - 5-B 9
Flying Horse Inn (A75) - 16-C11
Flying Horse Yard (e62) - 18-E16
Fook's Court (m97) - 18-E16
Fore Street - 39-J17
Foster Lane - 16-E11
Foster, Sir Reginald, House of (A31) - 25-G 9
Fountain Alley (h85) - 32-I 3
Fountain Court (i8) - 14-D 7
Fountain Court (h14) - 5-A10
Four Dove Alley (g85) - 30-G19
Four Swans Inn (B24) - 23-H 5
Fox and Goose Inn (A64) - 26-G11
Foxes Court (f25) - 25-G 9
Fox Horn Court (a14) - 28-F15
Fox Inn (A51) - 16-E12
Fox Ordinary Court (125) - 40-J19
Foxwell Court (c63) - 35-I10
Frederick, Sir John, House of (B51) - 24-F 7
Freeman's Yard (i68) - 11-E 2
French Alley (a79) - 37-I13

French Church (B62) - 27-G14
French Court (h44) - 27-G14
French Ordinary Court (160) - 30-I18
Fresh Wharf (n27) - 31-K15
Friar Street (k63) - 34-I 7
Friday Street - 25-H10
Fryer's Lane (m60) - 36-J12
Frying Pan Alley, Red Cross St. (c86) - 15-D10
Frying Pan Alley, Cow Cross (c42) - 13-D 5
Frying Pan Alley, Turnmill St. (b37) - 12-C 4
Frying Pan Alley, Golden Lane (a25) - 5-A 9
Frying Pan Alley, Petticoat Lane (d53) - 19-D17
Frying Pan Alley, St John St. (b54) - 13-C 6
Frying Pan Yard (k7) - 30-H19
Fuller's Rents (e95) - 21-F 1
Furnival's Inn - 22-F 3
Galley Quay (n49) - 31-K17
Garden Alley (d40) - 18-D16
Garden Alley (b48) - 13-C 5
Garlick Hill - 36-J11
Garter Court (b67) - 15-C 9
General Post Office (B59) - 28-G15
Gentleman Porter's Alley (d59) - 20-D20
George Alley, Birchin Lane (n59) - 27-H14
George Alley, Bishopsgate (c6) - 18-C16
George Alley, Aldgate (h72) - 29-G18
George Alley, Shoe Lane (g52) - 23-G 5
George Alley, Clerkenwell (a3) - 3-A 5
George Alley, Perpool Lane (c31) - 11-D 2
George Alley, Turnmill St. (b40) - 12-C 4
George Alley, Thames St. (n21) - 37-K13
George Alley, Seacoal Lane (g57) - 23-G 6
George Inn (A55) - 13-E 6
George Inn (A99) - 25-F 9
George Inn (A92) - 23-F 5
George Lane (m78) - 38-J15
George Street (g92) - 25-G 9
George Street - 20-C20
George Yard, Lombard St. (174) - 27-H14
George Yard, Whitechapel (e80) - 20-E20
George Yard, Moorfields (d30) - 17-D14
George Yard, Saffron Hill (d79) - 12-E 4
George Yard, Golden Lane (a95) - 5-B 9
George Yard, Snow Hill (i22) - 23-F 5
George Yard, Thames St. (m31) - 35-J 9
George Yard, Bow Lane (i57) - 26-H11
Gerard's Hall Inn (C16) - 25-H 9
Giltpur Street - 24-F 7
Girdlers' Hall (A63) - 16-E11
Glass House Yard (a86) - 4-B 8
Glass House Yard (k62) - 33-I 6
Glean Alley (e40) - 37-J14
Globe Alley (m73) - 26-H11
Globe Court (i6) - 4-B 8

Glovers' Hall (A20) - 15-C10
Glovers' Hall Court (b75) - 15-C10
Goat Alley (a28) - 5-A10
Goat Alley (n53) - 40-K20
Goat Yard (a27) - 5-A 9
Goat Yard (i29) - 23-H 6
Godfrey's Court (h10) - 25-G10
Golden Leg Court (154) - 26-H11
Golden Lion Inn (A32) - 13-D 6
Golden Lion Inn (A19) - 15-C 9
Golding Lane - 5-A 9
Gold's Alley (a75) - 3-B 6
Goldsmith's Alley (c78) - 15-D 9
Goldsmiths' Hall (B39) - 26-F11
Goldsmith Street - 25-G10
Goldman's Yard (i99) - 25-G10
Goose Alley (n58) - 30-H19
Goose Alley (151) - 25-H10
Goswell Street - 4-B 8
Gracechurch Street - 28-H15
Grange Inn (B94) - 31-I 1
Grant's Quay (n28) - 31-K15
Grasshopper Alley (c90) - 15-C10
Grasshopper Alley (b76) - 15-C10
Grasshopper Yard (c68) - 14-D 7
Gravel Alley (c68) - 11-E 2
Gravel Lane (d55) - 29-F18
Gray's Inn - 21-F 1
Gray's Inn Lane - 11-D 1
Great Bear Alley (g55) - 23-G 6
Great Bear Quay (n43) - 31-K16
Great Dice Quay (n35) - 31-K16
Great Eastcheap - 37-I14
Great Oxford Court (187) - 28-F16
Great Pearl Street - 9-A18
Great Rutland Court (m15) - 34-J 7
Great St Helens - 28-G16
Great St Thomas Apostle - 36-I11
Great Somer's Quay (n32) - 31-K15
Great Sword Bearer Alley (b85) - 6-B11
Great Tower Hill - 30-I18
Green Arbour Court (m78) - 23-G 6
Green Arbour Court (m88) - 39-J17
Green Court (h21) - 26-G12
Green Dragon Alley (n14) - 31-K 1
Green Dragon Court, Bread Street Hill (m36) - 35-J10
Green Dragon Court, Snow Hill (g63) - 23-G 6
Green Dragon Court, Thames St. (m26) - 35-J 9
Green Dragon Court, Cow Lane (126) - 26-H11
Green Dragon Court, Old Change (139) - 23-G 6
Green Dragon Court, Giltspur St. (135) - 23-F 6
Green Dragon Inn (B25) - 28-F15
Green Dragon Inn (A41) - 16-E12
Green Lettice Lane (i41) - 37-J13
Green's Rents (k55) - 23-H 5
Green Yard (a5) - 5-A10
Gloucester Court (a32) - 4-B 8

Greyfriars (g74) - 24-G 7
Greyhound Alley (e84) - 20-E20
Greyhound Court (199) - 31-J 2
Greyhound Court (f45) - 25-F 9
Greyhound Court (d82) - 13-E 5
Greyhound Inn (A79) - 13-E 6
Greyhound Inn (A54) - 14-C 8
Grey, Lord, House of (A14) - 20-E20
Grid Iron Alley (e91) - 8-A16
Griffin's Alley (a44) - 26-H12
Grocer's Alley (i59) - 26-H12
Grocers' Hall (B53) - 26-H11
Grub Street - 16-D11
Guildhall - 26-F11
Gully Hole (n26) - 31-K14
Gun Alley (d21) - 16-D12
Gunpowder Alley (i91) - 29-H18
Gunpowder Alley (i5) - 22-H 4
Gun Yard, Tower Hill (177) - 40-J20
Gun Yard, St Katharines (n52) - 40-K20
Gun Yard, Petticoat Lane (d52) - 19-D17
Gun Yard, Houndsditch (g8) - 29-F18
Gun Yard, Norton Folgate (b14) - 8-B16
Gutter Lane - 25-G10
Haberdashers' Hall (B8) - 16-D11
Half Moon Alley, Whitecross St. (c96) - 24-H 7
Half Moon Alley, Ludgate (i30) - 23-G 6
half Moon Alley, Moorfields (d24) - 16-D12
Half Moon Alley, Bishopsgate (d36) - 31-K16
Half Moon Court (c24) - 18-D16
Half Moon Court (g29) - 11-D 2
Half Moon Court (18) - 30-F20
Hall Court - 36-H11
Haman's Alley (h49) - 18-E15
Hamond's Quay (n30) - 32-J 3
Hand Alley, Strand (184) - 28-G15
Hand Alley, Moorfields (c2) - 31-J 1
Hand Alley, Bishopsgate - 6-B11
Hand Alley, Wormwood St. (155) - 30-I18
Hand and Hatchet Alley (167) - 17-C14
Hand and Hollybush Alley (188) - 18-D16
Hand and Pen Alley (c34) - 18-E15
Hand Court (e25) - 40-I19
Hand Court (a24) - 31-J 1
Hand Yard (m64) - 12-D 3
Hanging Sword Alley (k43) - 15-E10
Hanging Sword Court (k47) - 36-I12
Hare Court - 23-G 6
Hares Alley (c17) - 32-I 4
Harp Alley, Shoe Lane (i10) - 35-J 9
Harp Alley, Moor Lane (d18) - 23-F 6
Harp Alley, Cornhill (i69) - 27-H14
Harp Alley, Saffron Hill (c36) - 12-D 4
Harp Lane - 38-I16
Harris's Rents (a45) - 8-A16
Harrow Alley, Petticoat Lane (e68) - 19-E18
Harrow Alley, Aldersgate (f46) - 25-F 9

King's Head Court, Shoe Lane

- Harrow Alley, Whitechapel (n37) - 40-J20
- Harrow Alley, Tower Hill (n7) - 23-G6
- Harrow Alley, Fleet Lane (g58) - 3-A5
- Hart Alley (a4) - 23-H5
- Hart Court (i20)- 35-19
- Hart Court (k91) - 16-D12
- Harts Horn Alley (d22) - 35-I10
- Harts Horn Court (k97) - 5-A9
- Harts Horn Court (a17) - 24-F7
- Harts Horn Inn (A96) - 15-E10
- Hart Street- 39-I17
- Hart Street- 29-F18
- Hatchet Alley (g11) - 12-E4
- Hatton Court (d74) - 27-G14
- Hatton Court (h47) - 12-D3
- Hatton Garden - 12-C3
- Hatton Wall - 16-E12
- Helmet Court (e38) - 34-J8
- Helmet Court (m21) - 31-J2
- Hemlocks Court (k15) - 20-E19
- Hemp Yard (e77) - 32-I3
- Hen and Chicken Court (k33) - 29-F18
- Hendrijck's Yard (g7)- 32-I3
- Hercules Pillars Alley (k36) - 29-F18
- Hern, Sir Nathaniel, House of (B54) - 30-H19
- Heydon House (C21)- 13-C6
- Heydon's Yard (i95) - 13-E6
- Hicks' Hall- 16-E12
- Hide's Rents (d90) - 22-H4
- Hind Alley (e34) - 2-B3
- Hind Court (i1) - 7-A13
- Hockley Hole - 22-F3
- Hog Lane - 23-F5
- Holborn - 34-J7
- Holborn Bridge - 34-J7
- Holborn Hill - 30-G19
- Holiday Court - 31-J1
- Holiday Yard (k70) - 16-D11
- Holy Trinity Church, Minories (B70) - 37-I14
- Holywell Street - 15-E9
- Honeysuckle Court (d4) - 23-F5
- Hooker's Court (i26) - 40-K20
- Horn Alley (e5)- 31-K17
- Horn Alley (i17)- 5-B10
- Horn Alley (n51) - 27-G14
- Horn Court (n47)- 17-C14
- Horseshoe Alley, Golden Lane (a98) - 20-C19
- Horseshoe Alley, Threadneedle St. (i46) - 15-D10
- Horseshoe Alley, Petticoat Lane (e74)- 19-E18
- Horseshoe Alley, Moorfields (c3) - 19-D16
- Horseshoe Alley, Bishopsgate (d33) - 31-I1
- Horseshoe Alley, Fashion St. (c15)
- Horseshoe Alley, Whitecross St. (c95)
- Horseshoe Alley, Petticoat Lane (e74)
- Horseshoe Alley, St Clements Lane (k11)

- Horseshoe Alley, Crutched Friars (192) (89) - 28-F16
- Horseshoe Alley, Crutched Friars (192) - 29-H18
- Horseshoe Alley, Moor Lane (d14) - 16-D11
- Horseshoe Court (d91) - 13-E6
- Horseshoe Court (f34) - 24-F7
- Horseshoe Court (m86) - 38-J16
- Horse Yard (e31) - 16-E11
- Hosier Lane - 23-F6
- Houndsditch - 29-F17
- Housewife's Alley (d50) - 18-D15
- Hoyle's Court (f48) - 25-F9
- Huggin Alley (m38) - 35-J10
- Huggin Lane - 25-G10
- Huggin Lane (m45) - 35-J10
- Hugh's Court (m8) - 16-D11
- Huit's Rents (d5) - 38-J16
- Idle Lane - 38-I15
- Ingram's Court (138) - 32-J3
- Inner Temple - 36-J12
- Innholders' Hall (C4) - 34-J7
- Ireland Court (k72) - 34-J7
- Ireland Yard (k71) - 26-G11
- Ironmonger Lane - 29-H17
- Ironmongers' Hall (B91) - 23-G5
- Isaac's Rents (g46) - 24-G8
- Ivy Lane - 12-C4
- Jack Alley (b44) - 35-I10
- Jack Alley (19) - 34-J7
- Jackson's Court (m12) - 15-D10
- Jacob and his Twelve Sons Inn (A46) - 13-D5
- Jacob's Court (c43) - 15-C10
- Jacob's Well Alley (b72) - 40-J20
- Jenning's Rents (n9) - 38-I15
- Jerusalem Alley (147) - 15-D9
- Jewin Street - 15-C10
- John Baptist Court (b82) - 26-G11
- Joiners' Hall (C37) - 36-J12
- Joyner's Court (g9) - 29-F18
- Katherine Wheel Alley (b8) - 8-B15
- Katherine Wheel Alley (f21) - 23-F5
- Katherine Wheel Alley (e89) - 20-E20
- Katherine Wheel & George Alley (c14) - 11-C2
- Katherine Wheel Yard (d94) - 37-J14
- Katherine Wheel Yard (178) - 33-J6
- Katherine Wheel Yard (b27) - 26-G12
- Kifits' Court (m76) - 26-G11
- King Edward Street - 28-G16
- King's Arms Court (h16) - 23-F5
- King's Arms Inn (B65) - 32-J4
- King's Arms Inn (A90) - 8-B15
- King's Bench Walk - 19-D17
- King's Head Alley (b8)
- King's Head Alley (d54)

- King's Head Court, Golden Lane (a23) - 22-H4
- King's Head Court, Beech Lane (b73) - 5-A9
- King's Head Court, Shoreditch (a51) - 15-C10
- King's Head Court, St Martin le Grand (g84) - 8-A16
- King's Head Court, Carter Lane (k83) - 25-G9
- King's Head Court, Fish Street (m72) - 34-I8
- King's Head Court, Goswell St. (a78) - 37-J14
- King's Head Court, Gutter Lane (h3) - 4-B8
- King's Head Inn (A53) - 25-G10
- King's Head Inn (C14) - 13-E6
- King's Head Inn (A49) - -35-I9
- King's Head Yard (d72) - 11-E2
- King's Printing House - 12-E3
- King Street - 34-I7
- Kirby Street - 26-G11
- Knightrider Street - 12-D3
- Labour in Vain Yard (m24) - 34-I8
- Lad Lane - 35-J9
- Lamb Alley, Abchurch Lane (121) - 25-G10
- Lamb Alley, Old Change (i41) - 37-I13
- Lamb Alley, Bishopsgate (c10) - 25-H9
- Lamb Alley, Saffron Hill (d76) - 18-C16
- Lamb Court - 12-E4
- Lamb Court (k93) - 10-B19
- Lamb Court (122) - 35-I9
- Lambeth Hill - 37-I13
- Lamb Inn (C28)- 35-J9
- Lamb's Alley (e13) - 31-J1
- Lamb's Court (e12) - 15-E10
- Last Alley (c51) - 13-D5
- Laurence Lane - 26-G11
- Laurence Pountney Hill - 37-J13
- Laurence Pountney Lane - 37-J13
- Lawrence, Sir John, House of (B67) - 28-G16
- Leadenhall Street - 28-G16
- Leather Lane - 12-D3
- Leathersellers' Hall - 28-F16
- Lee's Yard (a66)- 2-B3
- Leg Alley (a50)- 8-A16
- Leopard Alley (c71) - 11-E2
- Leveret's Alley (a7) - 4-A8
- Lilipot Alley (h63) - 29-G17
- Lily Pot Lane - 25-F9
- Lime Street- 28-H16
- Lincoln's Inn - 21-G1
- Lincoln's Inn Fields - 21-H1
- Lion's Quay (n31) - 31-K15
- Liquor Pond Street - 11-C1
- Little Bear Alley (g56) - 23-G6
- Little Bear Quay (n42) - 31-K16

- Little Britain - 34-F8
- Little Bush Lane- 37-J13
- Little Carter Lane - 35-19
- Little Cheapside (m53) - 36-J11
- Little Dice Quay (n36) - 31-K16
- Little Distaff Lane - 35-19
- Little Duke's Place (h57) - 29-G17
- Little Eastcheap - 38-I15
- Little Elbow Lane - 36-J12
- Little Green Arbour Court (g66) - 23-G6
- Little Moorfields- 16-D12
- Little Old Bailey- 23-G6
- Little Oxford Street (88) - 28-F16
- Little Pearl Street - 9-A18
- Little Rutland Court (m14) - 34-J7
- Little St Helens - 28-F16
- Little Sheere Lane - 31-I2
- Little Somers Quay (n33) - 31-K15
- Little Tower Hill- 40-I20
- Little Trinity Lane - 35-J10
- Lock Alley (k27)- 31-I2
- Lombard Street - 27-H13
- London House (A5)- 14-E8
- London House Yard (134) - 24-H8
- London Wall - 17-E13
- Long Alley (a43) - 8-A15
- Long Entry (k60) - 33-I6
- Long Lane- 14-D7
- Loom Alley (e54) - 18-E15
- Lorimers' Hall (A78) - 16-E11
- Lothbury - 27-G13
- Love Lane - 25-F10
- Love Lane - 38-J15
- Lovell's Court (g79) - 24-G8
- Love's Court (g54) - 23-G5
- Lowman's Rents (b49) - 13-C5
- Ludgate Hill - 23-H6
- Ludgate Street - 24-H7
- Lutheran Church - 35-I10
- Madock's Rents (f51) - 25-F9
- Magpie Alley (e61) - 18-E16
- Magpie Inn (B32) - 22-G3
- Magpie Yard - 22-G3
- Maidenhead Alley, Grub St. (b96) - 28-G16
- Maidenhead Alley, Grays Inn (d62) - 28-G16
- Maidenhead Alley, Strand (186) - 12-D3
- Maidenhead Alley, Moor Lane (d17) - 28-F16
- Maidenhead Court, Aldersgate (e7) - 29-G17
- Maidenhead Court, Wood St. (f58) - 25-F9
- Maidenhead Court, St Thomas Apostle (112) - 28-H16
- Maidenhead Court, Maiden Lane (n56) - 21-G1
- Maidenhead Inn (C9) - 21-H1
- Maidenhead Yard (d29) - 31-K15

- Maidenhead Yard (d16) - 16-D11
- Maiden Lane - 25-F10
- Maiden Lane - 36-J11
- Mark Lane - 39-J17
- Martin's Court (d88) - 13-E5
- Martin's Rents (a47) - 8-A16
- Massey's Court (m81)- 38-J16
- Meeting House Yard (m75) - 37-J14
- Mercers' Court (m98) - 39-J17
- Mercers' Hall (B82) - 26-H11
- Merchant Taylors' Hall - 27-G14
- Merchant Taylors' School (C39)- 37-J13
- Mermaid Court (i33) - 24-H7
- Mermaid Inn (C8) - 34-I8
- Merryfield's Rents (g61) - 23-G6
- Michael's Alley (i70) - 27-H14
- Middle Street - 14-D8
- Middle Temple - 32-J3
- Middle Temple Lane - 32-J3
- Milford Alley - 31-J2
- Milk Street - 25-G10
- Milk Yard (i18) - 23-H5
- Miller's Court (e27) - 16-E11
- Mill Yard (a83) - 38-I16
- Mincing Lane - 30-H19
- Minories - 3-B6
- Mitre Court (e94) - 35-J10
- Mitre Court (m37) - 32-J3
- Mitre Court (k34) - 16-C12
- Mobb's Yard (b98) - 25-G9
- Moldmaker Row (g93) - 23-G5
- Molin's Rents (g45) - 10-A19
- Monmouth Street - 34-F8
- Montague Court (f42) - 20-D20
- Montague Street (d58) - 37-J14
- Monument, The- 17-E14
- Moorfields - 16-D11
- Moor Lane- 8-B16
- Moor's Alley (b12) - 16-E12
- Moor's Court (e36) - 35-I9
- Moor's Yard (k94) - 22-H4
- Morecroft's Court (h96) - 27-G13
- Morris, John, House of (h39) - 18-D16
- Morris, John, Property of (145) - 38-I15
- Moseley's Court (145) - 20-E19
- Moses and Aaron's Alley (e92) - 9-B17
- Moutague Court (a18) - 36-J12
- Mugget's Place (m64) - 15-E10
- Mugwell Street - 25-G10
- Munford's Court (h8) - 25-G10
- Mutton Court (g99) - 12-C4
- Mutton Lane
- Nag's Head Alley (c20) - 11-D1
- Nag's Head Court (h38) - 27-G13
- Nag's Head Court 129 - 37-J14
- Nag's Head Court (129) - 23-F6
- Nag's Head Inn (A72) - 17-E14
- Nag's Head Inn (A77) - 20-E20
- Nag's Head Inn (B28) - 29-F17
- Naked Boy Court (n13) - 31-K1
- Navy Office (C26) - 39-I17

Neptune Court (d27) - - - 17-D14
Nettleton Court (e8) - - 15-E9
Neville's Alley (g38) - - 22-G3
New Canal (formerly Fleet River) - 23-H5
Newcastle, Duke of, House of (A6) - 2-B4
Newcastle Street - 23-G5
New Court (i50) - 25-H10
New Court (e29) - 16-E11
New Court (h35) - 27-G13
New Fashion Street - 19-C18
New Fish Street - 37-J14
Newgate Street - 24-G7
New Inn - 31-J1
Newman's Rents (m46) - 36-J11
Newman's Yard (i71) - 27-H14
New Prison Walk - 2-A4
New Rents (g89) - 25-G9
New Street - 14-D8
New Street - 22-G4
New Street (k66) - 34-I7
Noble Street - 25-F9
Northumberland Alley (189) - 29-H18
Northumberland Court (f5) - 21-F2
Norton Folgate - 8-B16
Nun Alley (a52) - 8-A16
Nunnery Court (h13) - 25-G10
Oat Lane - 25-F9
Old Bailey - 25-G8
Old Change - 25-H9
Old Fish Street - 35-I9
Old Fish Street Hill - 35-J9
Old Jewry - 26-G12
Old Street - 4-A8
Old Street - 37-K13
Old Swan Lane - 13-E6
Old Yard (d83) - 24-G7
Oxford Arms Inn (B35) - 24-H7
Oxford Arms Inn (B78) - 24-F7
Oxford Arms Inn (A97) - 36-J11
Painter Stainers' Hall - 25-G9
Panyer Alley (g82) - 29-H17
Papillon, Thomas, House of (C54) - 25-F10
Parish Clerks' Hall (B4) - 30-F19
Parrot Alley (g15) - 11-D2
Parr's Rents (c22) - 33-I5
Parsons Court (k54) - 24-H8
Paternoster Row - 24-H8
Paul's Alley (135) - 15-D9
Paul's Alley (c83) - 34-I8
Paul's Bakehouse Court (k82) - 34-I8
Paul's Chain - 34-J8
Paul's Wharf - 14-E8
Paved Alley (e3) - 29-G18
Paved Alley (h69) - 25-G10
Paved Alley (156) - 11-D2
Paved Court (h1) - 21-F2
Paved Court (f2) - 16-C11
Paviors Court (b94) - 27-F14
Pay Office (B22) - 27-F14

Peacock Court (g28) - 30-F20
Peacock Inn (A43) - 14-D8
Peacock Yard (197) - 31-J2
Peahen Court (182) - 28-F15
Pelican Court (f41) - 34-F8
Perpool Lane - 11-D2
Peterborough Court (i5) - 23-H5
Peter's Alley (c57) - 13-D6
Peter's Lane (c58) - 13-D6
Petticoat Lane - 19-D17
Petty Canons (i37) - 24-H8
Petty Canons' Court (136) - 24-H8
Petty France - 18-E15
Pewter Platter Inn (A8) - 3-B6
Pheasant Court (d97) - 13-E6
Philip Lane - 15-E10
Philpot Lane - 38-I15
Phoenix Court (a77) - 4-B8
Phoenix Court (k88) - 35-I9
Phoenix Court (g73) - 24-G7
Physicians' College (B37) - 24-G7
Pickaxe Alley (152) - 39-I17
Pincock Alley (f37) - 24-F7
Pincock Lane (g78) - 24-G8
Pinder of Wakefield Alley (d63) - 11-E2
Pink's Alley (g39) - 22-G3
Pinners' Hall - 27-F14
Pissing Alley (183) - 31-J1
Pissing Alley (k39) - 32-I3
Pissing Alley (b52) - 13-C6
Plasterers' Hall (B6) - 25-F10
Playhouse Yard (B66) - 15-C9
Plough Alley, Whitechapel (e82) - 20-E20
Plough Alley, Tower Hill (n5) - 40-J20
Plough Alley, St Clements Lane (k8) - 31-I1
Plough Alley, Barbican (b64) - 15-C9
Plough Court, Golden Lane (a18) - 5-A9
Plough Inn (B95) - 31-I1
Plough Yard, Grays Inn (d64) - 11-E2
Plough Yard, Holborn Hill (f14) - 23-F5
Plough Yard, Fetter Lane (g36) - 22-G3
Plough Yard, Aldgate (h71) - 29-G18
Plough Yard, Houndsditch (f92) - 29-F17
Pope's Head Alley (i60) - 27-H13
Pope's Head Court (k17) - 31-J2
Pope's Yard (k6) - 30-H19
Poppinge Alley (i16) - 23-H5
Porter's Alley (f64) - 26-F11
Porter's Alley (a92) - 5-B9
Porter's Alley (b10) - 8-B16
Porter's Quay (n44) - 31-K17
Postern, The (B90) - 16-E12
Post Inn (B90) - 28-H16
Poultry - 26-H12
Poultry Compter (B83) - 16-C12
Powel's Alley (b77) - 34-I8
Prerogative Court (k78) - 34-I8
Prerogative Office (C6) - 40-I19
Preston's Yard (168) - 25-G9
Priest Court (g96) - 27-F14

Priest's Alley (m82) - 38-J16
Priest's Alley (n1) - 39-J18
Prigeons Court (122) - 23-H6
Primrose Alley (b15) - 8-B16
Printing House Lane (k63) - 33-I6
Pudding Lane - 38-J15
Puddle Dock Hill - 34-I7
Pump Court - 32-J3
Pump Yard (m94) - 35-J10
Pump Yard (c92) - 11-D2
Purse Alley (e93) - 16-E11
Purse Court (142) - 25-H9
Pye Corner - 24-F7
Queenhithe - 35-J10
Queen's Arms Yard (g51) - 23-G5
Queen's College Yard (m11) - 34-J7
Queen's Head Alley (e56) - 18-E15
Queen's Head Alley (g80) - 24-G8
Queen Street - 36-J11
Rainbow Court (c71) - 14-D8
Ralph's Quay (n38) - 31-K16
Ram Alley (k40) - 32-I4
Ram Inn (A37) - 13-D6
Rat Alley (132) - 16-D11
Rayns's Yard (f31) - 37-I14
Red Bull Alley (n17) - 24-F7
Red Bull Court (e32) - 37-K13
Red Bull Yard - 16-E11
Red Cow Alley (166) - 3-A5
Red Cow Alley (a12) - 40-I19
Red Cow Yard (b26) - 4-A8
Red Cross Alley, Little Britain (f43) - 11-C2
Red Cross Alley, Thames St. (n24) - 34-F8
Red Cross Alley, Strand (192) - 31-I1
Red Cross Alley, Jewin St. (c81) - 15-C9
Red Cross Alley, Aldgate (h83) - 5-A9
Red Cross Court (m95) - 30-G19
Red Cross Court (g71) - 39-J17
Red Cross Street - 24-G7
Red Hart Inn (B34) - 15-D10
Red Lion Alley, St Katharines (n12) - 22-H4
Red Lion Alley, Cow Cross (c48) - 20-C20
Red Lion Alley, Aldersgate St. (c75) - 13-D5
Red Lion Alley, Bishopsgate St. (c12) - 18-C16
Red Lion Alley, Minories (174) - 40-I19
Red Lion Court, Wood St. (e20) - 15-E10
Red Lion Court, Fleet St. (h95) - 22-H4
Red Lion Court, Brick Lane (d57) - 20-D19
Red Lion Court, Houndsditch (g5) - 29-F17
Red Lion Court, London Wall (e42) - 16-E12
Red Lion Court, Spitalfields (a58) - 9-A18

Red Lion Court, Bow Lane (k96) - 35-I10
Red Lion Court, Cock Lane (130) - 23-F6
Red Lion Inn, Red Cross St. (A21) - 15-C10
Red Lion Inn, Aldersgate St. (A16) - 14-C8
Red Lion Inn, Fleet St. (B75) - 22-H4
Red Lion Inn, Whitechapel (A76) - 20-E20
Red Lion Inn, Bishopsgate (A24) - 19-C17
Red Lion Inn, Chiswell St. (A22) - 16-C11
Red Lion Inn, Grays Inn (A26) - 11-D1
Red Lion Yard (g24) - 30-F19
Red Lion Yard (c70) - 14-D8
Rednal's Rents (b28) - 12-C3
River Street - 30-I18
Robin Hood Court, Thames St. (m28) - 35-J9
Robin Hood Court, Grub St. (b93) - 16-C11
Robin Hood Court, Shoe Lane (g41) - 22-G4
Robin Hood Court, Bow Lane (17) - 36-I11
Robinson's Court (h11) - 25-G10
Rolls - 37-I14
Rood Lane - 38-I15
Rope Makers Alley (b99) - 16-C12
Rose Alley, Golden Lane (a88) - 5-B9
Rose Alley, Leadenhall St. (h55) - 29-G17
Rose Alley, Bishopsgate St. (d49) - 18-D16
Rose Alley, Shoreditch (a46) - 8-A16
Rose Alley, Turnmill St. (b38) - 12-C4
Rose Alley, Spitalfields (a56) - 9-A18
Rose and Crown Alley (a11) - 4-A8
Rose and Crown Court, Whitecross St. (b79) - 15-C10
Rose and Crown Court, Perpool Lane (c27) - 11-D2
Rose and Crown Court, Shoe Lane (g53) - 23-G5
Rose and Crown Court, Fetter Lane (g34) - 22-G3
Rose and Crown Court, Foster Lane (g94) - 25-G9
Rose and Crown Court, Leadenhall St. (h63) - 29-G17
Rose Court (i48) - 13-C6
Rose Court (i56) - 25-H10
Rose Inn (A91) - 26-H11
Rose Inn (A52) - 39-J17
Rose Lane - 23-F5
Rosemary Branch Alley (180) - 13-E6
Rosemary Lane (f33) - 20-D19
Rosemary Lane - 40-I20
Rotten Row - 24-F7
Round Court (g90) - 40-I20
Round Hoop Court (b4) - 4-A8
Royal Exchange - 25-G9
Royal Oak Alley (194) - 5-B10

Sabb's Quay (n41) - - - 31-K16
Saddlers' Hall (B41) - - 25-G9
Saffron Hill - 12-D4
St Alban Wood Street, Church of - 25-F10
St Alphage, Church of - 16-E11
St Andrew by the Wardrobe, Church of - 34-I7
St Andrew Holborn, Church of - 22-F4
St Andrew's Court (f11) - 22-F4
St Andrew Undershaft, Church of (B66) - 28-G16
St Anne Aldersgate, Church of - 25-F9
St Anne Blackfriars, Church of - 34-I7
St Anne's Alley (f53) - 25-F9
St Ann's Lane - 25-F9
St Anthony, Church of - 36-I11
St Augustine Watling Street, Church of - 25-H9
St Bartholomew by the Exchange, Church of - 27-G13
St Bartholomew Court (f32) - 24-F7
St Bartholomew's Hospital - 24-F7
St Bartholomew the Great, Church of - 14-E7
St Bartholomew the Less, Church of - 14-E7
St Benet Fink, Church of - 27-G14
St Benet Gracechurch - 38-I15
St Benet Paul's Wharf, Church of - 5-B9
St Benet Sherehog, Church of - 26-H12
St Botolph Aldersgate, Church of - 25-F9
St Botolph Aldgate, Church of - 29-F18
St Botolph without Bishopsgate, Church of - 18-E16
St Bride (St Bridget), Church of - 33-I5
St Christopher le Stocks, Church of - 27-H13
St Clement Eastcheap, Church of - 37-I14
St Clement's, Back-side of - 31-J1
St Clement's Court (h9) - 25-G10
St Clement's Danes, Church of - 31-J2
St Clement's Lane - 31-I1
St Clement's Lane - 37-I14
St Dunstan in the East, Church of - 38-J16
St Dunstan in the West, Church of - 32-I3
St Dunstan's Court (m84) - 38-J16
St Dunstan's Hill - 38-J16
St Edmund Lombard Street, Church of - 27-H14
St Ethelburga, Church of, - 28-F16
St George Botolph Lane, Church of (C40) - 38-J15
St Giles Cripplegate, Church of - 15-D10
St Helen's Church - 28-G16
St James Garlickhithe, Church of - 36-I11
St John Baptist Court (k12) - 31-I1
St John's Alley (118) - 36-I12
St John's Court (d85) - 13-E5
St John's Court - 3-B5
St John's Court (m20) - 34-J8
St John's Lane - 13-C6
St John Street - 3-B5

Entry	Ref
St John the Baptist, Church of	36-I12
St John Zachary, Church of	25-F 9
St Katherine Coleman, Church of	29-H17
St Katherine Gree Church (B68)	29-G17
St Katherine's	40-K20
St Katherine's Lane	40-J20
St Lawrence Pountney, Church of	37-J13
St Lawrence Jewry, Church of	26-G11
St Leonard Eastcheap, Church of	37-J14
St Leonard Foster Lane, Church of	25-G 9
St Magnus the Martyr, Church of (C59)	31-K14
St Margaret Lothbury, Church of	26-G12
St Margaret Pattens, Church of	38-I16
St Martin Ironmonger Lane, Church of	26-G11
St Martin le Grand	25-G 9
St Martin Ludgate, Church of	24-H 7
St Martin Orgar, Church of	37-J14
St Martin Outwich, Church of (B60)	28-G15
St Martin's Lane	37-J13
St Martin Vintry, Church of	36-J11
St Mary Abchurch, Church of	37-I13
St Mary Aldermanbury, Church of	26-F11
St Mary Aldermary, Church of	36-I11
St Mary at Hill	38-J15
St Mary at Hill, Church of (C43)	38-J15
St Mary Axe	36-I12
St Mary Bothaw, Church of	25-H10
St Mary le Bow, Church of	35-J 9
St Mary Mounthaw, Church of	35-J 9
St Mary Somerset, Church of	25-F10
St Mary Staining, Church of	25-H10
St Matthew Friday Street, Church of	25-H10
St Matthew's Court (i47)	26-F11
St Michael Bassishaw, Church of	27-H14
St Michael Cornhill, Church of	37-J14
St Michael Crooked Lane, Church of	36-J12
St Michael Paternoster Royal, Church of	35-J10
St Michael Queenhithe, Church of	37-J14
St Michael's Lane	25-G10
St Michael Wood Street, Church of (B45)	35-I10
St Mildred Bread Street, Church of	26-H12
St Mildred Poultry, Church of (B84)	37-I14
St Nicholas Acon, Church of	37-I14
St Nicholas Alley (123)	35-I 9
St Nicholas Cole Abbey, Church of	37-I14
St Nicholas Lane	39-I17
St Olave Hart Street, Church of (C27)	39-I17
St Olave Jewry, Church of	26-G11

Entry	Ref
St Olave Silver Street, Church of	15-E 9
St Pancras Lane	26-H11
St Pancras Soper Lane, Church of	26-H11
St Paul's Cathedral	24-H 8
St Paul's Churchyard	25-H 9
St Paul's Lane	38-I15
St Peter Cornhill, Church of	28-H15
St Peter le Poor, Church of	27-F14
St Peter Paul's Wharf, Church of	35-J 9
St Peter's Alley (i13)	27-H14
St Peter's Hill	35-J 9
St Peter Westcheap, Church of	25-H10
St Sepulchre, Church of	23-F 6
St Size Lane	25-H12
St Stephen Coleman Street, Church of	26-G12
St Stephen Walbrook, Church of	36-J12
St Swithin's Lane	37-I13
St Thomas Apostles, Back of	36-I11
St Vedast, Church of (C23)	25-G 9
Salters' Hall (C23)	37-I13
Saracen's Head Inn, Leadenhall St. (B68)	29-G18
Saracen's Head Inn, Cheapside (B41)	25-H 9
Saracen's Head Inn, Snow Hill (A93)	23-F 6
Saracen's Head Inn, Carter Lane (C12)	35-I 9
Saracen's Head Yard (186)	38-F16
Satchel Alley (a37)	5-A10
Scalding Alley (i60)	26-H12
Scallop Court (k74)	34-I 7
Scotch Hall (C2)	33-I 6
Scotch Yard (m65)	37-J13
Scot's Yard (a33)	5-A10
Scriveners' Hall (B2)	22-F 4
Scroop's Court (f12)	29-F17
Scummer Alley (i96)	23-G 6
Seacoal Lane	39-J17
Seething Lane	32-I 3
Serjeants' Inn (B97)	32-I 4
Serjeants' Inn	15-D10
Serpent Alley (c85)	24-G 7
Sessions House	16-C11
Seven Star Alley (b90)	16-D11
Seven Step Alley (e75)	19-E18
Sharp's Alley (h51)	28-G16
Sharp's Alley (b13)	8-B16
Sharp's Alley (c44)	13-D 5
Sheere Lane	31-I 2
Sheers' Yard (e70)	19-E18
Sheldon, Sir Joseph, House of (C7)	34-I 8
Shepherd's Alley (i24)	23-H 6
Sherborne Lane	37-I13
Shew's Alley (a9)	32-I 3
Ship Court (k31)	27-G13
Ship Court (h39)	23-H 6
Ship Court (123)	5-A10
Shipley's Alley (a29)	26-G1

Entry	Ref
Shipley's Yard (194)	30-H19
Ship Yard, Red Cross St. (c87)	15-D10
Ship Yard, Cripplegate (e14)	15-E10
Ship Yard, Golden Lane (a26)	5-A 9
Ship Yard, Norton Folgate (b16)	8-B16
Ship Yard, Minories (h86)	30-G19
Shoe Lane	22-G 4
Shoreditch	9-A17
Shorter's Court (h36)	27-G13
Shovel Court (h5)	25-G10
Shute's Court (e30)	16-E11
Silver Street	15-E10
Sion College (A61)	16-E11
Sion Court (e26)	15-E10
Six Clerks' Office (B72)	21-H 2
Skinners' Hall (C33)	36-J12
Skinners' Rents (b17)	8-B16
Slaughterhouse Yard (k21)	31-J 2
Slaughter Yard (k9)	31-I 1
Small Beer Alley (b29)	12-C 3
Small Cole Alley (b51)	13-C 6
Smart's Quay (n34)	31-K16
Smithfield	14-E 7
Smock Alley	19-D18
Snead's Rents (c30)	11-D 2
Snow Hill	23-F 6
Snows Alley (a42)	7-A13
Soaper's Alley (d32)	18-D16
Soaper's Alley (a38)	5-B10
Soaper's Yard (190)	28-F16
Somerset House	21-F 2
Southampton Buildings	21-F 1
Southampton Court (e98)	23-G 5
Spectacle Alley (g47)	9-B18
Spitalfields	31-I 2
Spread Eagle Court (k20)	11-E 2
Spread Eagle Court	28-H15
Spread Eagle Yard (197)	20-E20
Squirrel Alley (197)	30-H19
Staining Lane	25-F10
Star Alley (a53)	39-J17
Star Alley (m89)	9-A17
Starch Alley (a6)	39-J17
Star Court Strand (k25)	4-A 8
Star Court Old Fish St. (k98)	31-I 2
Star Court Cornhill (h50)	35-I 9
Star Court Cheapside (i46)	28-G15
Star Court Bread St. (i49)	25-H 9
Star Inn (C41)	25-H10
Star Yard (14)	37-J14
Stationers' Hall	35-I10
Stephen's Court (b22)	24-H 7
Stew Lane (m42)	10-B19
Still Alley (e58)	12-C 4
Still Alley (e64)	35-J10
Still Alley (e78)	18-E16
Still Yard (n2)	19-E17
Still Yard (c4)	40-J19
Stone Alley (n54)	17-C14
Stone Court (h2)	25-G10

Entry	Ref
Stone Court (f44)	25-F 9
Stonecutter Street	23-G 5
Strand	31-J 1
Strand Bridge Lane	31-K 1
Strangeway Street	12-D 4
Strawberry Court (114)	36-I11
Suffolk Lane	37-J13
Sugar Baker's Yard (h56)	29-G17
Sugar Loaf Alley, Fenchurch St. (i85)	29-H17
Sugar Loaf Alley, Mark Lane (155)	39-I17
Sugar Loaf Alley, Moor Lane (d10)	16-D11
Sugar Loaf Alley, Milford Lane (m1)	31-J 2
Sugar Loaf Alley, Leadenhall St. (h60)	29-H17
Sugar Loaf Alley, Smithfield (c55)	13-D 6
Sugar Loaf Alley, Spitalfields (b21)	10-B19
Sugar Loaf Alley, Wentworth St. (d56)	20-D19
Sugar Loaf Court, Perpool Lane (c25)	11-D 2
Sugar Loaf Court, Distaff Lane (l1)	35-I 9
Sugar Loaf Court, Garlick Hill (m47)	36-J11
Sugar Loaf Court, Moor Lane (d77)	16-D11
Sugar Loaf Court, Saffron Hill (d25)	12-E 4
Sun Alley, Cow Cross (c47)	13-D 5
Sun Alley, Grub St. (b92)	16-C11
Sun Alley, St John St. (a73)	3-B 6
Sun Alley, Petticoat Lane (e72)	19-E18
Sun Alley, St Clements Lane (k10)	31-I 1
Sun and Trumpet Alley (g13)	29-F18
Sun Court, Chick Lane (d86)	13-E 5
Sun Court, St John St. (a71)	3-B 6
Sun Court, Golden Lane (b69)	15-C10
Sun Court, Cornhill (n60)	27-H14
Sun Dial Court (d25)	17-D14
Sutton's Court (f13)	22-F 4
Sutton Street	4-A 7
Swan Alley, Golden Lane (a22)	5-A 9
Swan Alley, Coleman St.	26-F12
Swan Alley, Broad St. (81)	28-F15
Swan Alley, Whitechapel (g25)	30-F19
Swan Alley, Smithfield (c59)	13-D 6
Swan Alley, Minories (198)	30-H19
Swan Court (m96)	39-J17
Swan Court (k23)	31-I 2
Swan Court (138)	25-H 9
Swan Inn (A89)	23-F 5
Swan Inn (A5)	9-A17
Swan Inn (A45)	15-D 9
Swan with Two Necks Inn (B11)	13-D 6
Swan with Two Necks Inn (A31)	13-D 6
Swan with Two Necks Inn (A87)	23-F 5

Entry	Ref
Swan Yard (g72)	24-G.7
Swan Yard (d38)	18-D16
Swadland Court (182)	40-J20
Swithin's Alley (h45)	27-G14
Sword and Buckler Court (125)	23-H 6
Symond's Inn (B71)	21-H 2
Talbot Court (a48)	8-A16
Talbot Court (148)	38-I15
Talbot Inn (C46)	31-K 1
Tallow Chandlers' Hall (C22)	36-I12
Tarr Alley (h78)	29-G18
Temple Church	32-J 3
Tennis Court Lane (m59)	36-J12
Tennis Court Yard (f6)	21-F 2
Tenter Alley (d20)	16-D12
Thames Street	34-J 8
Thanet House (A58)	15-E 9
Thatch Alley (d84)	13-E 5
Thavie's Inn (A86)	22-F 4
Thrapston's Court (k44)	32-I 4
Thread Needle Alley (d28)	17-D14
Threadneedle Street	27-G14
Three Arrow Inn (A78)	21-F 1
Three Bowl Alley (e90)	20-E20
Three Bowl Court (g6)	29-F17
Three Colts Inn (A4)	7-A14
Three Cranes Lane (m55)	36-J11
Three Crown Alley (95)	29-F17
Three Crown Court (h77)	29-G18
Three Crown Court (a59)	9-A18
Three Crown Court (m48)	36-J11
Three Cup Court (g81)	24-G 8
Three Cups Inn (C15)	35-I10
Three Cups Inn (A12)	13-C 6
Three Cups Inn (A15)	14-C 8
Three Dagger Alley (i40)	25-H 9
Three Dagger Alley (e92)	15-D10
Three Diamond Court (n62)	23-F 6
Three Falcon Court (13)	22-H 4
Three Fox Court (c65)	14-D 7
Three Fox Court (127)	37-I14
Three Herrings Court (b77)	15-C10
Three Horseshoe Alley (g35)	22-G 3
Three Horseshoe Court (c66)	14-D 7
Three Horseshoe Inn (A9)	4-B 8
Three King Court, Whitecross St. (a99)	5-B10
Three King Court, Minories (h84)	30-G19
Three King Court, Lombard St. (128)	
Three King Court, Fleet St. (h99)	37-I14
Three Kings Alley (193)	22-H 4
Three Leg Alley (h92)	31-J 2
Three Leg Court (93)	22-H 3
Three Link Alley (c18)	15-D10
Three Malt Men Court (b3)	20-C20
Three Nun Alley (i62)	5-B10
Three Nun Inn (B30)	27-H13
Three Pigeon Alley (b65)	29-F18
Three Pigeon Alley (e47)	15-C 9
	17-E13

Three Pigeon Alley (a68) - 2-B 3
Three Pigeon Court (c79) - 15-D 9
Three Tun Alley, Cow Cross (c53) - 13-D 5
Three Tun Alley, Petticoat Lane (e71) - 19-E18
Three Tun Alley, Bishopsgate St. (d35) - 18-D16
Three Tun Alley, London Wall (e50) - 17-E13
Three Tun Alley, Thames St. (m74) - 37-J14
Three Tun Alley, Newgate St. (g76) - 24-G 8
Throgmorton Street - 27-G14
Throll Street - 20-C20
Timber Street - 35-J10
Titus Court (d78) - 12-E 4
Tobacco Roll Court (i78) - 28-H15
Tokenhouse Garden - 27-G13
Tower Ditch - 40-J20
Tower Hill - 30-I18
Tower Royal Court (137) - 36-I11
Tower Street - 39-J17
Townsend Lane - 35-J10
Towns End - 2-B 3
Trig Lane - 35-J 9
Trinity Court (e11) - 15-E 9
Trinity Court (m39) - 35-J10
Trinity House (C45) - 39-J17
Trinity Lane - 35-J10
Tripe Yard (g19) - 30-F19
Tudor Street - 33-J 6
Tulce, Sir Henry, House of (B55) - 27-F13
Turk's Head Alley (e98) - 21-F 1
Turk's Head Court (a87) - 5-B 9
Turnagain Lane - 23-F 5
Turner's Alley (f28) - 23-F 6
Turner's Alley (143) - 38-I15
Turn Mill Street - 12-C 4
Turnwheel Lane - 36-I12

Two Brewers Yard (a20) - 5-A 9
Two Cranes Court (h94) - 22-H 3
Unicorn Alley (d7) - 16-D11
Unicorn Alley (a55) - 9-A18
Vine Court, Temple - 32-J 3
Vine Court, Thames St, (n46) - 31-K17
Vine Court, Turnmill St. (b31) - 12-C 4
Vine Court, Bishopsgate - 18-D16
Vine Court, Shoe Lane (i12) - 23-H 5
Vine Court, Broad St. (179) - 28-F15
Vinegar Yard (b50) - 13-C 6
Vine Inn (B23) - 28-F15
Vine Street- - 12-C 3
Vine Street- - 9-B18
Vine Yard (b55) - 14-C 8
Vine Yard (a97) - 5-B10
Vintners' Hall - 36-J11
Vyner, Sir Robert, House of (B85) - 27-H13
Walbrook - 36-I12
Walls Court (172) - 40-I19
Walnut Tree Yard (e60) - 18-E16
Ward, Sir Patient, House of (C38) - 37-J13
Warnford Court (h34) - 27-G13
Warwick Court - 24-G 7
Warwick House - 21-F 1
Warwick Lane - 24-G 7
Water Lane - 39-J17
Water Lane- - 32-J 4
Water Lane- - 32-J 4
Waterman, Sir George, House of (C57) - 37-J13
Watermen's Hall (C58) - 37-K13
Water Street - 33-J 6
Watling Street - 25-H 9
Wax Chandlers' Hall (B43) - 25-G 9
Weavers' Hall (B13) - 26-F11
Weaver's Yard (190) - 31-J 2
Weeden's Rents (k5) - 30-H19

Weigh House Yard (i72) - 27-H14
Well Alley (h87) - 30-G19
Well Alley (153) - 39-I17
Well Alley (f19) - 23-F 5
Well Court (i58) - 26-H11
Well Yard (d98) - 14-E 7
Well Yard (g58) - 23-G 6
Wentford Street - 20-D19
Westbury Street - 9-A18
West Harding Street - 22-G 4
Whalebone Court (h27) - 27-G13
Wharf's Alley (c49) - 13-D 5
Wheatsheaf Alley (h62) - 29-G17
Wheatsheaf Alley (a74) - 3-B 6
Wheatsheaf Alley (n23) - 31-K14
Wheeler's Alley (170) - 40-I19
Wheeler's Street- - 9-B18
Whistler's Court (119)- - 37-J13
Whitchurch House (C53) - 29-H17
White Bear Alley (g12) - 29-F18
White Bear Court (m13) - 34-J 7
White Bell Alley (131)- - 37-I14
Whitechapel - 30-F19
White Cock Alley (n20) - 37-K13
White Cock Court (k95) - 35-I10
Whitecross Street - 5-A10
White Foot Alley (b33) - 12-C 4
Whitefriars - 32-I 4
White Hart Alley (b47) - 12-C 4
White Hart Court (e59) - 18-E16
White Hart Court (g31) - 30-F19
White Hart Inn, Coleman St. (B16) - 26-F12
White Hart Inn, London Wall (A71) - 17-E14
White Hart Inn, St.John St. (A1) - 3-A 5
White Hart Inn, Leather Lane (A29) - 11-D 2
White Hart Yard (g12) - 29-F18
White Hind Court (d34) - 18-D16
White Hind Yard (c91) - 15-D10

White Horse Alley, Turnmill St. (b42) - 12-C 4
White Horse Alley, Bishopsgate (f85) - 28-F15
White Horse Alley, Barbican (b59) - 14-C 8
White Horse Alley, Cow Cross (c50) - 13-D 5
White Horse Alley, Old St. (a10) - 4-A 8
White Horse Alley, Holborn (f9) - 22-F 3
White Horse Alley, Strand (185) - 31-J 1
White Horse Alley, Whitechapel (174) - 13-D 5
White Horse Court (f77) - 30-F19
White Horse Court (195) - 28-F15
White Horse Inn, Cripplegate (A62) - 31-J 2
White Horse Inn, Fetter Lane (B33) - 15-E10
White Horse Inn, Coleman St. (C53) - 22-G 3
White Horse Inn, Barbican (A17) - 14-C 8
White Horse Inn, Fleet St. (B76) - 26-F12
White Horse Inn, London Wall (A68) - 22-H 4
White Horse Yard, Broad St. (f78) - 17-E13
White Horse Yard, Aldersgate St. (b56) - 25-G10
White Horse Yard, St.John St. (A36) - 14-C 8
White Horse Yard, Tower Hill (179) - 3-A 5
White Lion Alley (187) - 40-J20
White Lion Court, Cripplegate (e41) - 31-J 1
White Lion Court, Fleet St. (k48) - 16-E12
White Lion Court, Charterhouse Lane (c64) - 33-I 5
White Lion Court, Coleman St. (f68) - 14-D 7
White Lion Court, Aldersgate St. (b6) - 26-F12
- 14-C 8

White Lion Yard, Cow Lane (f24) - 23-F 6
White Rose Alley (b78) - 16-C11
White Rose Court (f71) - 26-F12
White's Alley (f70) - 26-F12
White's Alley (g33) - 21-G 2
White's Alley (f8) - 22-F 3
White's Alley (d19) - 16-D12
White Swan Yard (a69) - 2-B 3
Wiggin's Quay (n39) - 31-K16
Williams Alley (b9) - 8-B16
Winchester Court (e18) - 15-E10
Winchester Street (174) - 27-F14
Windgoose Court (m63) - 36-J12
Windmill Alley (f18) - 23-F 5
Windmill Alley (b35) - 12-C 4
Windmill Alley (173) - 40-I19
Windmill Alley (e81) - 20-E20
Windmill Court (k28) - 31-I 2
Windmill Court (g64) - 23-G 6
Windmill Inn (A30) - 13-D 6
Windmill Inn (A81) - 23-F 5
Wine Office Court (i2) - 22-H 4
Winston's Court (e21) - 15-E10
Woodruffe Lane- - 30-I18
Wood Street - 25-F10
Wood Street Compter (B46) - 25-G10
Wooley's Court (157) - 25-F10
Wool Pack Alley (e65) - 19-E17
Woolpack Inn (A36) - 13-D 6
Worcester Place (m51) - 36-J11
Worley's Court (k61) - 33-I 6
Wormwood Street - 18-E15
Wrestler's Court (e52) - 17-E13
Wych Street - 31-J 1

Yellow Court (h88) - 30-G19
Yokely's Yard (n6) - 40-J20
Young's Quay (n40) - 31-K16

Detail of a border for Ogilby and Morgan's map of the City of London, 1676, taken from a unique surviving sheet of 'ornaments'. The design draws attention to Charles II's patronage. (Reproduced by courtesy of Guildhall Library.)

SYMBOL INDEX

The allocation of the same symbol to two different place names and the omissions from the symbol sequences result from errors in Ogilby and Morgan's *Explanation*, which it was not practicable to correct.

Boundary markings

The wavy line on the map pages indicates the extent of the Great Fire, 1666. The broad black line is the City wall. The chain represents the boundary of the City. o o o o represents the boundary of the wards. A pricked line represents the boundaries of the parishes and liberties.

Ref	Entry
B29-	Crown Inn, Aldgate
B30-	Three Nun Inn
B31-	Blue Boar Inn
B32-	Magpie Inn
B33-	White Horse Inn, Fetter Lane
B34-	Davis, Sir Thomas, House of
B34-	Red Hart Inn
B35-	Oxford Arms Inn
B36-	Bell Inn, Warwick Lane
B37-	Physicians' College
B38-	Crown Inn, Warwick Lane
B39-	Goldsmiths' Hall
B40-	St Vedast, Church of
B41-	Saddlers' Hall
B41-	Saracen's Head Inn, Cheapside
B43-	Wax Chandlers' Hall
B45	St Michael Wood Street, Church of
B46-	Wood Street Compter
B47-	Cross Keys Inn, Wood St.
B48-	Blossoms Inn
B49-	Blackwell Hall
B51-	Frederick, Sir John, House of
B52-	Clayton, Sir Robert, House of
B53-	Grocers' Hall
B54-	Hern, Sir Nathaniel, House of
B55-	African House
B57-	Tulce, Sir Henry, House of
B58-	Drapers' Hall
B59-	General Post Office
B60-	St Martin Outwich, Church of
B61	Barnardiston, Sir Samuel, House of
B62-	French Church
B65-	King's Arms Inn
B66	St Andrew Undershaft, Church of
B67-	Lawrence, Sir John, House of
B68-	St Katherine Cree Church
B68	Saracen's Head Inn, Leadenhall St.
B70-	Holy Trinity Church, Minories
B71-	Symond's Inn
B72-	Six Clerks' Office
B73-	Chancery Office
B74-	Bond's Stables
B75-	Red Lion Inn, Fleet St.
B76-	White Horse Inn, Fleet St.
B77-	Belle Savage Inn
B78-	Oxford Arms Inn
B80-	Bell Inn, Friday St.
B82-	Mercers' Hall
B83-	Poultry Compter
B84-	St Mildred Poultry, Church of
B85-	Vyner, Sir Robert, House of
B86-	Cross Keys Inn, Gracechurch St.
B87-	Spread Eagle Inn
B88-	East India House
B90-	Post Inn
B91-	Ironmongers' Hall
B94-	Grange Inn
B95-	Plough Inn
B97-	Serjeants' Inn
B98-	Bolt and Tunn Inn
B99-	Black Horse Inn
C1-	Apothecaries' Hall
C2-	Scotch Hall
C4-	Innholders' Hall
C5-	Dean of St Paul's House
C6-	Prerogative Office
C7-	Sheldon, Sir Joseph, House of
C8-	Mermaid Inn
C9-	Maidenhead Inn
C10-	Doctors' Commons
C12-	Saracen's Head Inn, Carter Lane
C14-	King's Head Inn
C15-	Three Cups Inn
C16-	Gerard's Hall Inn
C18-	Black Lion Inn
C20-	Bell Inn, Walbrook
C21-	Cutlers' Hall
C21-	Heydon House
C22-	Tallow Chandlers' Hall
C23-	Salters' Hall
C25-	Clothworkers' Hall
C26-	Navy Office
C27-	St Olave Hart Street, Church of
C28-	Lamb Inn
C29-	Blacksmiths' Hall
C30-	Bell Inn, Fish St. Hill
C33-	Skinners' Hall
C35-	Chequer Inn
C37-	Joiners' Hall
C38-	Ward, Sir Patient, House of
C39-	Merchant Taylors' School
C40	St George Botolph Lane, Church of
C41-	Star Inn
C43-	St Mary at Hill, Church of
C45-	Trinity House
C46-	Talbot Inn
C47-	Dyers' Hall
C48-	Fishmongers' Hall
C50-	Cooks' Hall
C52-	Bricklayers' Hall
C53-	Whitchurch House
C54-	Papillon, Thomas, House of
C57-	Waterman, Sir George, Hse of
C58-	St Magnus the Martyr, Church of
C59-	Excise Office
C60-	Bottle of Hay Yard
a2-	George Alley, Clerkenwell
a3	Hart Alley
a4-	Green Yard
a5-	Starch Alley
a6-	Leveret's Alley
a7-	Crooked Billet Alley
a8-	Shew's Alley
a9-	White Horse Alley, Old St.
a10-	Rose and Crown Alley
a11-	Red Cow Alley
a12-	Cup Court
a13-	Fox Horn Court
a14-	Basket Yard
a15-	Carpenter's Yard, Golden Lane
a16-	Harts Horn Court
a17-	Moutague Court
a18-	Plough Alley, Golden Lane
a19-	Chequer Court
a20-	Two Brewers Yard
a21-	Chequer Yard
a22-	Swan Alley, Golden Lane
a23-	King's Head Court, Golden Lane
a24-	Hand Court
a25-	Frying Pan Alley, Golden Lane
a26-	Ship Yard, Golden Lane
a27-	Goat Yard
a28-	Goat Alley
a29-	Shipley's Alley
a32-	Gloucester Court
a33-	Scott's Yard
a34-	Bear and Ragged Staff Yard
a35-	Chequer Alley
a36-	Adam and Eve Alley
a37-	Satchel Alley
a38-	Soaper's Alley
a42-	Snows Alley
a43-	Long Alley
a44-	Griffin's Alley
a45-	Harris's Rents
a46-	Rose Alley, Shoreditch
a47-	Martin's Rents
a48-	Talbot Court
a49-	Bowl Court
a50-	Leg Alley
a51-	King's Head Court, Shoreditch
a52-	Nun Alley
a53-	Star Alley
a54-	Cross Keys Alley
a55-	Unicorn Alley
a56-	Rose Alley, Spitalfields
a58-	Red Lion Court, Spitalfields
a59-	Three Crown Court
a60-	Castle Alley, Spitalfields
a61-	Angel Alley, Smithfield
a64-	Council's Alley
a65-	Dickenson's Yard
a66-	Coulter's Yard
a67-	Lee's Yard
a68-	Adam's Yard
a69-	Three Pigeon Alley
a70-	White Swan Yard
a71-	Bull Head Alley
a72-	Sun Court, St John St.
a73-	Butcher's Alley
a74-	Sun Alley, St John St.
a75-	Wheatsheaf Alley
a76-	Gold's Alley
a77-	Carpenter's Yard, St John St.
a78-	Phoenix Court
a79-	King's Head Court, Goswell St.
a80-	Bell Alley, Goswell St.
a81-	Butcher's Arms Yard
a82-	Baker's Yard
a83-	Flying Horse Court
a84-	Currier's Yard
a85-	Fann's Alley
a86-	Glass Horn Yard
a87-	Turk's Head Court
a88-	Rose Alley, Golden Lane
a89-	Falconer's Alley
a90-	Ball Alley, Golden Lane
a91-	Ball Yard
a92-	Porter's Alley
a94-	Cupid's Alley
a95-	George Yard, Golden Lane
a96-	Angel Alley, Golden Lane
a97-	Vine Yard
a98-	Horseshoe Alley, Golden Lane
a99-	Three King Court, Whitecross St.
b1-	Cherry Tree Alley
b2-	Coopers' Alley
b3-	Three Malt Men Court
b4-	Round Hoop Court
b5-	Black Raven Court
b6-	Christopher Alley
b6-	White Lion Court, Aldersgate St.
b8-	Katherine Wheel Alley
b8-	King's Head Alley
b9-	Williams' Alley
b10-	Porter's Alley
b11-	Brown's Alley
b12-	Moor's Alley
b13-	Sharp's Alley
b14-	Gun Yard, Norton Folgate
b15-	Primrose Alley
b16-	Ship Yard, Norton Folgate
b17-	Skinners' Rents
b20-	Bell Alley, Spitalfields
b21-	Sugar Loaf Alley, Spitalfields
b22-	Stephen's Court
b25-	Dearing's Rents
b26-	Red Cow Yard
b27-	Katherine Wheel Yard
b28-	Rednal's Rents
b29-	Small Beer Alley
b30-	Bull Head Alley
b31-	Vine Court, Turnmill St.
b32-	Black Spread Eagle Alley
b33-	White Foot Alley
b34-	Cinnamon Alley
b35-	Windmill Alley
b36-	Bitt Alley
b37-	Frying Pan Alley, Turnmill St.
b38-	Rose Alley, Turnmill St.
b39-	Stewart's Alley
b40-	George Alley, Turnmill St.
b41-	Bell Alley, Turnmill St.
b42-	White Horse Alley, Turnmill St.
b43-	Block Alley
b44-	Jack Alley
b45-	Bell Alley, Turnmill St.
b46-	Cock Alley, Turnmill St.
b47-	White Hart Alley
b48-	Garden Alley
b49-	Lowman's Rents
b50-	Vinegar Yard
b51-	Small Cole Alley
b52-	Pissing Alley
b53-	Rose and Crown Yard
b54-	Frying Pan Alley, St John St.
b55-	Vine Yard
b56-	White Horse Yard, Aldersgate St.
b57-	Crown Yard
b58-	Devonshire Court
b59-	White Horse Alley, Barbican
b61-	Cannon Court
b63-	Fig Tree Court
b64-	Plough Alley, Barbican
b65-	Three Pigeon Alley
b66-	Playhouse Yard
b67-	Garter Court
b68-	Cock's Head Court
b69-	Sun Court, Golden Lane
b70-	Black Raven Court
b71-	Black Horse Alley, Golden Lane
b72-	Jacob's Well Alley
b73-	King's Head Court, Beech Lane
b74-	Barn Yard
b75-	Glovers' Hall Court
b76-	Grasshopper Alley
b77-	Powel's Alley
b77-	Three Herrings Court
b78-	White Rose Alley
b79	Rose and Crown Court, Whitecross St.
b80-	Angel Court, Red Cross St.
b81-	Castle Court, Whitecross St.
b82-	John Baptist Court
b83-	Bowling Alley
b85-	Great Sword Bearer Alley
b87-	Cross Dagger Court
b88-	Ball Alley, Grub St.
b89-	Broad Arrow Alley
b90-	Seven Star Alley
b91-	Five Inkhorn Court
b92-	Sun Alley, Grub St.
b93-	Robin Hood Court, Grub St.
b94-	Paviors Court
b95-	Bell Alley, Grub St.
b96-	Maidenhead Alley, Grub St.
b98-	Mobb's Yard
b99-	Rope Makers Alley
c2-	Hand Alley, Moorfields
c3-	Horseshoe Alley, Moorfields
c4-	George Alley, Bishopsgate
c6-	Acorn Alley
c7-	Cock Yard
c8-	Angel Alley, Bishopsgate
c9-	Lamb Alley, Bishopsgate
c10-	Bell Alley, Bishopsgate
c11-	Dunning's Alley
c12-	Katherine Wheel & George Alley
c13-	Horseshoe Alley, Fashion St.
c14-	Baily's Court
c15-	Hares Alley
c17-	Three Link Alley
c18-	Nag's Head Alley
c20-	Parr's Rents
c22-	Bradshaw's Buildings
c23-	U.S.M. Court

Ref.	Place
c25-	Sugar Loaf Court, Perpool Lane
c26-	Cock Alley, Perpool Lane
c27-	Rose and Crown Court, Perpool Lane
c28-	Crown Court, Perpool Lane
c30-	Snead's Rents
c31-	George Alley, Perpool Lane
c34-	Hand and Pen Alley
c35-	Bell Alley, Saffron Hill
c36-	Harp Alley, Saffron Hill
c37-	Bowling Alley
c38-	Black Lion Court
c40-	Flower de Luce Alley
c41-	Dagger Alley
c42-	Frying Pan Alley, Cow Cross
c43-	Jacob's Court
c44-	Sharp's Alley
c45-	Coffin Alley
c46-	Cradle Alley
c47-	Sun Alley, Cow Cross
c48-	Red Lion Alley, Cow Cross
c49-	Wharf's Alley
c50-	White Horse Alley, Cow Cross
c51-	Last Alley
c52-	Blind Beggar Alley
c53-	Three Tun Alley, Cow Cross
c54-	Black Horse Alley, Smithfield
c55-	Sugar Loaf Alley, Smithfield
c57-	Peter's Alley
c58-	Peter's Lane
c59-	Swan Alley, Smithfield
c60-	Castle Yard
c62-	Adam and Eve Alley
c63-	Foxwell Court
c64-	White Lion Court, Charterhouse Lane
c65-	Three Fox Court
c66-	Three Horseshoe Court
c67-	Carpenter's Court
c67-	Cradle Alley
c68-	Grasshopper Yard
c68-	Gravel Alley
c69-	Boarded Alley
c69-	Cat Alley
c70-	Baldwin's Court
c70-	Cradle Court
c71-	Leopard Alley
c71-	Rainbow Court
c72-	Black Horse Court
c75-	Red Lion Alley, Aldersgate St.
c76-	Cradle Court
c77-	Cockpit Yard
c78-	Goldsmith's Alley
c79-	Three Pigeon Court
c80-	Bull Head Court, Cripplegate
c81-	Red Cross Alley, Jewin St.
c82-	Crowder's Well Alley
c83-	Paul's Alley
c84-	Bear and Ragged Staff Alley
c85-	Serpent Alley
c86-	Frying Pan Alley, Red Cross St.
c87-	Ship Yard, Red Cross St.
c88-	Cock Alley, Cripplegate
c89-	Cock Yard
c90-	Grasshopper Alley
c91-	White Hind Yard
c92-	Pump Yard
c92-	Three Dagger Alley
c93-	Three Leg Court
c95-	Horseshoe Alley, Whitecross St.
c96-	Half Moon Alley, Whitecross St.
c97-	Cross Keys Court
c98-	Butler's Court
d1-	Flower de Luce Court, Grub St.
d2-	Flying Horse Court
d3-	Bell Alley, Grub St.
d4-	Honeysuckle Court
d5-	Huit's Rents
d6-	Clun's Alley
d7-	Clun's Yard
d8-	Unicorn Alley
d9-	Church Rents
d10-	Black Horse Alley, Cripplegate
d11-	Sugar Loaf Alley, Moor Lane
d12-	Carr Yard
d13-	Butler's Alley
d14-	Cock Alley, Moor Lane
d15-	Horseshoe Alley, Moor Lane
d16-	Bell Yard, Moor Lane
d17-	Maidenhead Yard
d18-	Maidenhead Alley, Moor Lane
d19-	Harp Alley, Moor Lane
d20-	White's Alley
d21-	Tenter Alley
d22-	Gun Alley
d23-	Harts Horn Alley
d24-	Angel Alley, Moorfields
d25-	Half Moon Alley, Moorfields
d26-	Sun Dial Court
d27-	Cock in Hole Court
d28-	Neptune Court
d29-	Thread Needle Alley
d30-	Maidenhead Yard
d31-	George Yard, Moorfields
d32-	Crooked Billet Yard
d33-	Soaper's Alley
d34-	Horseshoe Alley, Bishopsgate
d35-	White Hind Court
d36-	Three Tun Alley, Bishopsgate
d37-	Half Moon Alley, Bishopsgate
d38-	Crown Yard
d39-	Swan Yard
d40-	Bottle Alley
d49-	Garden Alley
d50-	Housewife's Alley
d51-	Rose Alley, Bishopsgate St.
d52-	Gun Yard, Petticoat Lane
d53-	Frying Pan Alley, Petticoat Lane
d54-	King's Head Alley
d55-	Gravel Lane
d56-	Sugar Loaf Alley, Wentworth St.
d57-	Red Lion Court, Brick Lane
d58-	Montague Street
d59-	Gentleman Porter's Alley
d60-	Angel Alley, Whitechapel
d61-	Burton's Rents
d62-	Maidenhead Alley, Grays Inn
d63-	Pinder of Wakefield Alley
d64-	Plough Yard, Grays Inn
d65-	Feathers Yard
d66-	Angel Alley, Grays Inn
d72-	King's Head Yard
d73-	Cockrel's Rents
d74-	Cross Keys Court
d75-	Blue Court
d76-	Lamb Alley, Saffron Hill
d77-	Sugar Loaf Court, Saffron Hill
d78-	George Yard, Saffron Hill
d79-	Blue Boar Court
d80-	Brewer's Yard
d81-	Greyhound Court
d82-	Old Yard
d83-	Thatch Alley
d84-	St John's Court
d85-	Sun Court, Chick Lane
d86-	Martin's Court
d88-	Cross Keys Court
d89-	Hide's Rents
d90-	Horseshoe Court
d91-	Church Yard Alley, Smithfield
d92-	Blue Boar Court
d93-	Katherine Wheel Yard
d94-	Boar's Head Court
d95-	Black Raven Court
d96-	Pheasant Lane
d97-	Well Yard
d98-	Paved Alley
e3-	Horn Alley
e5-	Angel Alley, Aldersgate St.
e6-	Maidenhead Court, Aldersgate
e7-	Nettleton Court
e8-	Deputy's Court
e9-	Ball Alley, Aldersgate St.
e10-	Trinity Court
e11-	Lamb's Court
e12-	Lamb's Alley
e13-	Ship Yard, Cripplegate
e14-	Bowyer's Court
e15-	Bib's Court
e16-	Doby Court
e17-	Winchester Court
e18-	Do Little's Yard
e19-	Red Lion Court, Wood St.
e20-	Winston's Court
e21-	Fell Court
e22-	Burges Court
e23-	Cock Court
e24-	Hand Court
e25-	Sion Court
e26-	Miller's Court
e27-	Bassishaw Court
e28-	New Court
e29-	Shute's Court
e30-	Horse Yard
e31-	Red Bull Court
e32-	Blackwell Hall Court
e33-	Hind Court
e34-	Moor's Court
e37-	Bradon's Court
e37-	Crown Court, London Wall
e38-	Helmet Court
e39-	Bishop's Court
e40-	Glean Alley
e41-	White Lion Court, Cripplegate
e42-	Red Lion Court, London Wall
e46-	Angel Alley, London Wall
e47-	Three Pigeon Alley
e48-	Ball Alley, London Wall
e49-	Boarded Entry
e50-	Three Tun Alley, London Wall
e52-	Crown Court, Moorfields
e53-	Loom Alley
e54-	Hand Alley, Wormwood St.
e55-	Queen's Head Alley
e56-	Cock Alley, Wormwood St.
e57-	Still Alley
e58-	White Hart Court
e59-	Walnut Tree Yard
e60-	Magpie Alley
e61-	Flying Horse Yard
e62-	Dolton's Yard
e63-	Still Alley
e64-	Wool Pack Alley
e65-	Bird in Hand Court
e66-	Cobb's Yard
e67-	Harrow Alley, Petticoat Lane
e68-	Bates's Yard
e69-	Sheers' Yard
e70-	Three Tun Alley, Petticoat Lane
e71-	Sun Alley, Petticoat Lane
e72-	Black Bell Alley
e73-	Horseshoe Alley, Petticoat Lane
e74-	Seven Step Alley
e75-	Bramble Alley
e76-	Hemp Yard
e77-	Still Alley
e78-	Black Bell Alley
e79-	George Yard, Whitechapel
e80-	Windmill Alley
e81-	Plough Alley, Whitechapel
e82-	Cock Alley, Whitechapel
e83-	Greyhound Alley
e84-	Spread Eagle Yard
e85-	Church Alley
e86-	Bell Alley, Whitechapel
e87-	Katherine Wheel Alley
e88-	Three Bowl Alley
e89-	Grid Iron Alley
e90-	Moses and Aaron's Alley
e91-	Purse Alley
e92-	Mitre Court
e93-	Fuller's Rents
e94-	Fleece Alley
e95-	Southampton Court
e97-	Turk's Head Alley
e98-	Baker's Alley
f1-	Paved Court
f2-	Fisher's Alley
f4-	Bishop's Head Court
f5-	Northumberland Court
f6-	Tennis Court Yard
f8-	White's Alley
f9-	White Horse Alley, Holborn
f10-	Bartlett's Court
f11-	St Andrew's Court
f12-	Scroop's Court
f13-	Sutton's Court
f14-	Plough Yard, Holborn Hill
f15-	Field Lane
f16-	Feathers Alley
f17-	Horn Alley
f18-	Windmill Alley
f19-	Well Alley
f20-	Beehive Alley
f21-	Katherine Wheel Alley
f22-	George Yard, Snow Hill
f23-	Bell Alley, Snow Hill
f24-	White Lion Yard, Cow Lane
f25-	Foxes Court
f26-	Green Dragon Court, Cow Lane
f27-	Bull Head Court, Cow Lane
f28-	Turner's Alley
f29-	Nag's Head Court
f30-	Red Lion Court, Cock Lane
f31-	Rayns's Yard
f32-	St Bartholomew Court
f33-	Rosemary Lane
f34-	Horseshoe Court
f35-	Church Lane
f35-	Green Dragon Court, Giltspur St.
f36-	Ball Court
f37-	Pincock Alley
f40-	Carpenter's Yard, Little Britain
f41-	Pelican Court
f42-	Montague Court
f43-	Red Cross Alley, Little Britain
f44-	Cross Keys Court
f45-	Stone Court
f46-	Greyhound Court
f47-	Harrow Alley, Aldersgate
f48-	Falcon Yard
f49-	Hoyle's Court
f50-	Fitchett's Court
f51-	Austine's Rents
f52-	Madock's Rents
f53-	Dyer's Alley
f54-	St Anne's Alley
f55-	Crown Court, Foster Lane
f56-	Paved Court
f57-	Wooley's Court
f58-	Maidenhead Court, Wood St.
f61-	Bassishaw Court
f62-	Carpenter's Yard, Aldermanbury
f63-	Dyer's Court
f64-	Porter's Alley
f65-	Chimney Alley
f68-	White Lion Court, Coleman St.
f69-	Cradle Alley
f70-	White's Alley

Index (cont.)

Code	Place
f71-	White Rose Court
f74-	Winchester Street
f75-	Austin Friars
f76-	Crown Court, Broad Street
f77-	White Horse Court
f78-	White Horse Yard, Broad St.
f79-	Vine Court, Broad St.
f80-	Bull Alley
f81-	Swan Alley, Broad St.
f82-	Peahen Court
f83-	Clark's Alley
f84-	Angel Court, Bishopsgate St.
f85-	White Horse Alley, Bishopsgate
f86-	Saracen's Head Yard
f87-	Great Oxford Street
f88-	Little Oxford Street
f89-	Horseshoe Alley, Camomile St.
f90-	Soaper's Yard
f91-	Axe Yard
f92-	Plough Yard, Houndsditch
f93-	Flower de Luce Court, Houndsditch
f94-	Cole's Yard
f95-	Three Crown Alley
f96-	Scummer Alley
f97-	Red Lion Court, Houndsditch
f98-	Three Bowl Court
g1-	Hendrijck's Yard
g2-	Castle Court, Houndsditch
g3-	Fire Ball Alley
g4-	Fire Ball Court
g5-	Cock and Hoop Yard
g6-	Crown Alley
g7-	Red Lion Court, Houndsditch
g8-	Gun Yard, Houndsditch
g9-	Joyner's Court
g11-	Hatchet Alley
g12-	White Bear Alley
g12-	White Hart Yard
g13-	Sun and Trumpet Alley
g14-	Black Bull Alley
g15-	Parrot Court
g16-	Church Lane
g16-	White Horse Alley, Whitechapel
g17-	Anchor and Hart Alley
g18-	Boar's Head Yard
g19-	Tripe Yard
g20-	Red Lion Yard
g24-	Swan Alley, Whitechapel
g25-	Blue Anchor Alley
g26-	Belle Sauvage Yard
g28-	Peacock Court
g28-	Half Moon Court
g29-	Eagle and Child Alley
g30-	White Hart Court
g31-	White's Alley
g33-	Rose and Crown Court, Fetter Lane
g34	Three Horseshoe Alley
g35-	Plough Alley, Fetter Lane
g36-	Church Yard Alley, Fetter Lane
g37-	Neville's Alley
g38-	Pink's Alley
g39-	

Code	Place
g40-	Box's Court
g41-	Robin Hood Court, Shoe Lane
g42-	Cockpit Court
g43-	Brown's Court
g44-	Falcon Court
g45-	Molin's Rents
g46-	Isaac's Rents
g47-	Spectacle Alley
g48-	Church Yard Alley, Shoe Lane
g49-	Eagle and Child Alley
g50-	Brewer's Yard
g51-	Queen's Arms Yard
g52-	George Alley, Shoe Lane
g53	Love's Court
g54-	Great Bear Alley
g55-	Little Bear Alley
g56-	George Alley, Seacoal Lane
g57-	Harrow Alley, Fleet Lane
g58-	Well Yard
g58-	Fisher's Rents
g60-	Merryfield's Rents
g60-	Cock Court
g61-	Green Dragon Court, Snow Hill
g62-	Windmill Court
g63-	Angel Court, Snow Hill
g64-	Little Green Arbour Court
g65-	Dunstan's Alley
g66-	Ellis Court
g67-	Brown's Court
g68-	Dean's Court
g69-	Red Cross Court
g70-	Swan Yard
g71-	Phoenix Court
g72-	Greyfriars
g73-	Baker's Court
g74-	Three Tun Alley, Newgate St.
g75-	Bull Head Court, Newgate St.
g76-	Pincock Lane
g77-	Lovell's Court
g78-	Queen's Head Alley
g79-	Three Cup Court
g80-	Panyer Alley
g81-	Dean's Court
g82-	King's Head Court, St Martin le Grand
g83-	Four Dove Alley
g84	Christopher Alley
g84	Cock Alley, St Martin le Grand
g85-	Baptist Alley
g86-	New Rents
g87-	Round Court
g88-	Flower de Luce Court, Foster Lane
g89-	George Street
g90-	Moldmaker Row
g91	Rose and Crown Court, Foster Lane
g92-	Dark Entry
g93-	Priest Court
g94	Mutton Court
g95-	Paved Court
g96-	Stone Court
g99-	King's Head Court, Gutter Lane
h1-	Day's Court
h2-	
h3-	
h4-	

Code	Place
h5-	Shovel Court
h7-	Coach and Horses Court
h8-	Munford's Court
h9-	St Clement's Court
h10-	Godfrey's Court
h11-	Robinson's Court
h12-	Feathers Court
h13-	Nunnery Court
h14-	Fountain Court
h15-	Castle Court, Milk St.
h16-	King's Arms Court
h21-	Banes's Yard
h21-	Green Court
h25-	Draper's Court
h27-	Whalebone Court
h32-	Angel Court, Throgmorton St.
h33-	Copthall Court
h34-	Warnford Court
h35-	New Court
h36-	Shorter's Court
h37-	Bartholomew Court
h38-	Nag's Head Court
h39-	Capel Court
h39-	Clayton, Sir Robert, House of
h39-	Morris, John, House of
h40-	Ship Court
h41-	Crown Court, Throgmorton St.
h42-	Adam Court
h43-	Cushion Court
h44-	Brittain's Yard
h45-	French Court
h45-	Swithin's Alley
h47-	Hatton Court
h48-	Crown Court, Threadneedle St.
h49-	Haman's Alley
h50-	Star Court Cornhill
h51-	Sharp's Alley
h54-	Creechurch Lane
h55-	Rose Alley, Leadenhall St.
h56-	Sugar Baker's Yard
h57-	Little Duke's Place
h58-	Black Raven Alley
h59-	Angel Alley, Leadenhall St.
h60-	Sugar Loaf Alley, Leadenhall St.
h61-	Axe Alley
h62-	Wheatsheaf Alley
h63-	Lillipot Alley
h63	Rose and Crown Court, Leadenhall St.
h64-	Billiter Court
h65-	Coleman's Yard
h66-	Clocker's Alley
h68-	Paved Alley
h69-	Petty Canons' Court
h71-	Plough Yard, Aldgate
h72-	George Alley, Aldgate
h73-	Swan Court
h75-	Bliss's Yard
h76-	Conduit Yard
h77-	Angel Court, Minories
h78-	Three Crown Court
h79-	Harrow Alley, Whitechapel
h80-	Bell Alley, Whitechapel

Code	Place
h81-	Chequer Yard
h82-	Black Boy Alley
h83-	Coach and Horses Court
h84-	Red Cross Alley, Aldgate
h85-	Three King Court, Minories
h86-	Fountain Alley
h87-	Ship Yard, Minories
h88-	Well Alley
h89-	Yellow Court
h91-	Feathers Alley
h92-	Bolt and Tun Alley
h93-	Three Leg Alley
h94-	Flower de Luce Alley
h94-	Carpenter's Yard, Aldgate
h95-	Two Cranes Court
h96-	Red Lion Court, Fleet St.
h97-	Morecroft's Court
h98-	Dunstan's Court
h99-	Bolt Court
i1-	Three King Court, Fleet St.
i2-	Hind Court
i3-	Wine Office Court
i4-	Three Falcon Court
i5-	King's Head Court, Shoe Lane
i5-	Gunpowder Alley
i6-	Peterborough Court
i7-	Globe Court
i8-	Ben Johnson's Court
i9-	Fountain Court
i10-	Angel Court, Shoe Lane
i11-	Harp Alley, Shoe Lane
i12-	Currier's Alley
i13-	Vine Court, Shoe Lane
i13-	Church Yard Alley, Shoe Lane
i16-	St Peter's Alley
i17-	Poppinge Alley
i18-	Black Horse Alley, Fleet St.
i19-	Milk Yard
i20-	Cock and Py Court
i20-	Flower de Luce Court, Fleet Court
i21-	Hart Court
i22-	Black and White Court
i23-	Prigeons Court
i24-	Ship Court
i25-	Shepherd's Alley
i27-	Sword and Buckler Court
i29-	Dolphin Court
i30-	Goat Yard
i31-	Half Moon Alley, Ludgate
i33-	Mermaid Court
i34-	London House Yard
i35-	Paul's Alley
i36-	Petty Canons' Court
i37-	Petty Canons
i38-	Swan Court
i39	Green Dragon Court, Old Change
i40-	Three Dagger Alley
i41-	Lamb Alley, Old Change
i42-	Purse Court
i43-	Crane Court
i44-	Blue Boar Court
i45-	Angel Court, Friday St.

Code	Place
i46-	Horseshoe Alley, Threadneedle St.
i46-	Star Court Cheapside
i47-	Rose Court
i48-	Star Court Bread St.
i49-	New Court
i50-	Goose Alley
i51-	Bird in Hand Alley
i51-	Golden Leg Court
i53-	Crown Court, Cheapside
i54-	Rose Court
i55-	George Yard, Bow Lane
i56-	Dove Court
i57-	Well Court
i58-	Grocer's Alley
i58-	Pope's Head Alley
i59-	Scalding Alley
i60-	Barge Yard
i60-	Three Nun Alley
i61-	Castle Alley, Cornhill
i62-	Castle Court, Cornhill
i63-	Exchange Alley
i64-	Dove Court
i66-	Freeman's Yard
i67-	Harp Alley, Cornhill
i68-	Michael's Alley
i69-	Newman's Yard
i70-	Weigh House Yard
i71-	George Yard, Lombard St.
i72-	Corbet Court
i74-	Bell Yard, Gracechurch St.
i75-	Boar's Head Court
i76-	Tobacco Roll Court
i77-	Ball Alley, Lime St.
i78-	Fenchurch Alley
i79-	Sugar Loaf Alley, Fenchurch St.
i80-	Northumberland Alley
i85-	Cock Alley, Crutched Friars
i89-	Gunpowder Alley
i90-	Horseshoe Alley, Crutched Friars
i91-	Shipley's Yard
i92-	Heydon's Yard
i94-	Brown's Alley
i95-	Squirrel Alley
i96-	Swan Alley, Minories
i97-	Goldman's Yard
i98-	Crown Court, Minories
i99-	Black Horse Court
k1-	Eales's Yard
k2-	Bell and Wheel Yard
k3-	Weeden's Rents
k4-	Pope's Yard
k5-	Frying Pan Yard
k6-	Plough Alley, St Clements Lane
k7-	Slaughter Yard
k8-	Sun Alley, St Clements Lane
k9-	St John Baptist Court
k10-	Hemlocks Court
k11	Pope's Head Court
k12-	Crown Court, Chancery Lane
k15-	
k16-	
k17-	
k19-	

Code	Place
k20-	Spread Eagle Court
k21-	Slaughterhouse Yard
k22-	Crown Court, Strand
k23-	Swan Court
k24-	Blue Anchor Court
k25-	Star Court Strand
k27-	Lock Alley
k28-	Windmill Court
k29-	Flying Horse Court
k30-	Bull Head Court, Fleet St.
k31-	Ship Court
k33-	Hen and Chicken Court
k34-	Mitre Court
k35-	Falcon Court
k36-	Hercules' Pillars Alley
k39-	Pissing Alley
k40-	Ram Alley
k41-	Bolt and Tun Court
k42-	Boar's Head Court
k43-	Hanging Sword Alley
k44-	Thrapston's Court
k45-	Essex Court
k46-	Ashen Tree Court
k47-	Hanging Sword Court
k48-	White Lion Court, Fleet St.
k49-	Bride's Alley
k54-	Parsons Court
k55-	Green's Rents
k56-	Bear Alley
k57-	Bear Yard
k60-	Long Entry
k61-	Worley's Court
k62-	Glass House Yard
k63-	Friar Street
k64-	Printing House Lane
k66-	Cobb's Court
k67-	New Street
k69-	Church Entry
k70-	Cotton Court
k71-	Holiday Yard
k72-	Ireland Yard
k73-	Ireland Court
k74-	Cloister Court
k75-	Church Alley
k76-	Scallop Court
k77-	Canterbury Court
k78-	Flower de Luce Court, Blackfriars
k79-	Chancellor's Rents
k80-	Prerogative Court
k81-	Black Swan Court
k82-	Bell Court
k83-	Bell Court
k85-	Paul's Bakehouse Court
k86-	King's Head Court, Carter Lane
k87-	Ashurst's Court
k88-	Buck's Head Court
k90-	Phoenix Court
k91-	Bull Head Yard
—	Hart Court

Code	Place
11-	Crane Court
12-	Lamb Court
14-	Moor's Yard
15-	White Cock Court
17-	Red Lion Court, Bow Lane
18-	Harts Horn Court
19-	Star Court, Old Fish St.
110-	Sugar Loaf Court, Distaff Lane
112-	Cradle Court
113-	Star Yard
114-	Brazile Yard
115-	Robin Hood Court, Bow Lane
116-	Half Moon Court
117-	Jack Alley
118-	Aldermary Churchyard
119-	Maidenhead Court, St Thomas Apostle
121-	Beehive Court
122-	Strawberry Court
123-	Blunderbuss Alley
124-	Bond's Court
125-	Dodson's Court
126-	St John's Alley
127-	Whistler's Court
128-	Lamb Alley, Abchurch Lane
129-	Lamb Court
130	St Nicholas Alley
131-	Bell Alley, Cannon St.
132-	Fox Ordinary Court
137-	Hooker's Court
138-	Three Fox Court
141-	Cross Keys Alley
143-	Nag's Head Court
144-	Three King Court, Lombard St.
145-	Church Yard Alley, Clements Lane
146-	White Bell Alley
147-	Rat Alley
148-	Tower Royal Court
149-	Ingram's Court
150-	St Paul's Court
151-	Turner's Alley
152-	Broven's Court
152-	Moseley's Court
153-	Crown Court, Gracechurch St.
154-	Jerusalem Alley
155-	Talbot Court
156-	Christal Court
157-	Dunstan's Court
158-	Bell Yard, Mincing Lane
159-	Burnt Yard
160-	Pickaxe Alley
160-	Well Alley
163-	Bell Wheel Alley
164-	Sugar Loaf Alley, Mark Lane
—	Crossley's Court
—	'Dyer's Court
—	Carr Yard
—	Crown Court, Crutched Friars
—	Brown's Court
—	French Ordinary Court
—	Allum Yard
—	Chain Alley

Code	Place
165-	Black and White Alley
166-	Red Cow Alley
167-	Hand and Hatchet Alley
168-	Preston's Yard
170-	Wheeler's Alley
172-	Walls Court
173-	Windmill Alley
174-	Red Lion Alley, Minories
175-	Blue Anchor Alley
176-	Bell Alley, Tower Hill
177-	Gun Yard, Tower Hill
178-	Katherine Wheel Yard
179-	White Horse Yard, Tower Hill
180-	Rosemary Branch Alley
181-	Child's Alley
181-	Culver Court
182-	Sweadland Court
183-	Pissing Alley
184-	Hand Alley, Strand
185-	White Horse Alley, Strand
186-	Maidenhead Alley, Strand
187-	White Lion Alley
188-	Hand and Hollybush Alley
189-	Crown Court, Strand
190-	Weaver's Yard
191-	Black Eagle Alley
192-	Red Cross Alley, Strand
193-	Three Kings Alley
194-	Royal Oak Alley
195-	White Horse Court
196-	Cross Keys Alley
197-	Peacock Yard
198-	Crown Court, Strand
199-	Greyhound Court
m1-	Sugar Loaf Alley, Milford Lane
m2-	Cresser's Court
m3-	Clothworkers' Court
m4-	Crown Court, Whitefriars
m8-	Hugh's Court
m9-	Banister's Court
m10-	Flower de Luce Alley
m11-	Queen's College Yard
m12-	Jackson's Court
m13-	White Bear Court
m14-	Little Rutland Court
m15-	Great Rutland Court
m16-	Common Lane
m17-	Dunghill Lane
m18-	Church Hill
m19-	Cradle Court
m20-	St John's Court
m21-	Helmet Court
m24-	Labour in Vain Yard
m25-	Black Boy Alley
m26	Green Dragon Court, Thames St.
m28-	Robin Hood Court, Thames St.
m29-	Castle Alley, Thames St.
m30-	Brooks's Yard
m31-	George Yard, Thames St.
m33-	Bell Alley, Thames St.

Code	Place
m35-	Five Foot Lane
m36	Green Dragon Court, Bread St. Hill
m37-	Mitre Court
m38-	Huggin Alley
m39-	Trinity Court
m40-	Cowden's Rents
m41-	Bowling Alley
m42-	Stew Lane
m43-	Dark Lane
m45-	Huggin Lane
m46-	Newman's Rents
m47-	Sugar Loaf Court, Garlick Hill
m48-	Three Crown Court
m51-	Worcester Place
m52-	Anchor Lane
m53-	Little Cheapside
m54-	Church Lane
m55-	Three Cranes Lane
m57-	Chequer Yard
m58-	Emperor's Head Lane
m59-	Tennis Court Lane
m60-	Fryer's Lane
m61-	Brewer's Lane
m62-	Double Hood Court
m63-	Windgoose Court
m64-	Hand Yard
m65-	Mugget's Place
m68-	Scotch Yard
m69-	Black Swan Alley
m71-	Artichoke Court
m72-	Bell Yard, Fish St.
m73-	King's Head Court, Fish Street
m74-	Globe Alley
m75-	Three Tun Alley, Thames St.
m76-	Meeting House Yard
m77-	Kiffits' Court
m78-	Fenn Court
m80-	George Lane
m81-	Botolph Alley
m82-	Massey's Court
m83-	Priest's Alley
m84-	Church Yard Alley, St Dunstan's Hill
m85-	St Dunstan's Court
m86-	Carpenter's Yard, Tower St.
m88-	Horseshoe Court
m89-	Green Arbour Court
m90-	Star Alley
m91-	Black Boy Alley
m92-	Crown Court, Seething Lane
m93-	Rose Court
m94-	Chittering Alley
m94-	Custom House Court
n.95-	Pump Yard
m96-	Red Cross Court
m97-	Fook's Court
m98-	Mercers' Court
m99-	Barking Yard
n1-	Priest's Alley
n2-	Still Yard

Code	Place
n4-	Blue Anchor Yard
n5-	Plough Alley, Tower Hill
n6-	Yokely's Yard
n7-	Harrow Alley, Tower Hill
n8-	Eagle and Child Alley
n9-	Blue Anchor Alley
n9-	Jenning's Rents
n11-	Ball Alley, St Katharines
n12-	Red Lion Alley, St Katharines
n13-	Naked Boy Court
n14-	Green Dragon Alley
n15-	Angel Court, Strand
n16-	Axe Yard
n17-	Campion Lane
n17-	Red Bull Alley
n18-	Clark's Alley
n19-	Angel Alley, Thames St.
n20-	White Cock Alley
n21-	George Alley, Thames St.
n22-	Black Raven Alley
n23-	Wheatsheaf Alley
n24-	Red Cross Alley, Thames St.
n25-	Church Yard Alley, Thames St.
n26-	Gully Hole
n27-	Fresh Wharf
n28-	Grant's Quay
n29-	Cox's Quay
n30-	Hamond's Quay
n31-	Lion's Quay
n32-	Great Somer's Quay
n33-	Little Somers Quay
n34-	Smart's Quay
n35-	Great Dice Quay
n36-	Little Dice Quay
n38-	Ralph's Quay
n39-	Wiggin's Quay
n40-	Young's Quay
n41-	Sabb's Quay
n42-	Little Bear Quay
n43-	Great Bear Quay
n44-	Porter's Quay
n45-	Custom House Quay
n46-	Vine Court, Thames St,
n47-	Horn Court
n49-	Chester Quay
n49-	Galley Quay
n50-	Brewer's Quay
n51-	Horn Alley
n52-	Gun Yard, St Katharines
n53-	Rose Court
n54-	Goat Alley
n55-	Stone Alley
n56	Cat's Hole
n57-	Maidenhead Court, Maiden Lane
n58-	Bell Alley, Smithfield
—	Goose Alley
n59-	George Alley, Birchin Lane
n60-	Sun Court, Cornhill
n62-	Three Diamond Court